A PRACTIC~ ~IIDE TO
COMMU~ L WORK
P~ ~É UK

~urbett

V~ ~ a guest chapter by
Jane Pye

P

First published in Great Britain in 2024 by

Policy Press, an imprint of
Bristol University Press
University of Bristol
1–9 Old Park Hill
Bristol
BS2 8BB
UK
t: +44 (0)117 374 6645
e: bup-info@bristol.ac.uk

Details of international sales and distribution partners are available at
policy.bristoluniversitypress.co.uk

© Bristol University Press 2024

British Library Cataloguing in Publication Data
A catalogue record for this book is available from the British Library

ISBN 978-1-4473-7099-4 paperback
ISBN 978-1-4473-7100-7 ePub
ISBN 978-1-4473-7101-4 ePdf

Cover design: Lyn Davies Design
Front cover image: scusi/Alamy
Bristol University Press and Policy Press use environmentally
responsible print partners.
Printed and bound in Great Britain by CPI Group (UK) Ltd,
Croydon, CR0 4YY

FSC
www.fsc.org
MIX
Paper | Supporting
responsible forestry
FSC® C013604

Contents

List of figures and tables

Figures

Tables

List of abbreviations

ABCD	Asset-based community development
ARBD	Alcohol-related brain damage
BASW	British Association of Social Workers
CCETSW	Central Council for Education and Training in Social Work
CLD	Community learning and development
CDP	Community development project
CSW	Community social work
DfE	Department for Education
DoH	Department of Health
GP	General Practitioner
GRTSWA	Gypsy, Roma and Traveller Social Work Association
HCPC	Health and Care Professions Council
HEI	Higher education institution
MDT	Multi-Disciplinary Team
NISCC	Northern Ireland Social Care Council
NISW	National Institute for Social Work
NHS	National Health Service
NPM	New public management
OBE	Order of the British Empire
PCF	Professional Capabilities Framework
SCW	Social Care Wales
SSSC	Scottish Social Services Council
SiSWE	Standards in Social Work Education
SWE	Social Work England
UK	United Kingdom
US/USA	United States (of America)
YMCA	Young Men's Christian Association

Glossary of keywords and terms

Action Research A research method, typically conducted from the inside rather than by external researchers, which aims to investigate, find a solution and then solve an issue.

Capitalism An economic system where the ownership of the means of production is centralised in the ownership and control of a minority, creating wage labour and inequality.

Care Management Often associated with assessment (as in 'Assessment and Care Management'), but an entirely separate concept. According to Harris and White (2018:256) care management, imported from the USA, describes 'an integrated and circular process for identifying and addressing the needs of individuals within available resources, which recognizes, at least rhetorically, that those needs are unique to the individuals concerned. First introduced by the community care reforms in the early 1990s, it comprised seven distinct stages: the publishing of information, determination of the level of assessment, assessment, care planning, implementation of the care plan, monitoring, and review.' In practice it has come to signify an approach that is procedural, assessment-driven, used to ration services, and often removed from ongoing relation-based practice where assessments are developed over time and in partnership with users. Care management implies a split between assessor/purchaser, and provider of services, so is associated with the marketisation of social work.

Casework (and Case Management) The traditional approach to social work service delivery within which social workers are allocated caseloads made up of individuals (and families) with whom they address issues on an individual basis.

Civil Society Two meanings: the popular one in the UK describes voluntary, community organisations and informal groups that come together to make communities better places to live. Gramsci (Italian Marxist philosopher 1891–1937) describes it as the public sphere where trade unions and political parties gain concessions from those with power his alternative description of the 'state'.

Co-design The involvement of stakeholders in a design process.

Co-production The involvement of stakeholders on an equal basis in making decisions about services and how they are run.

Community capacity building Enabling all members of a community, including the most disadvantaged, to develop skills and competencies that enable them to take control of their lives and contribute to local development.

Community development A process where community members come together to take collective action and generate solutions to common problems.

Community-orientation Social work activity within the context of the community within which the individual service user has membership.

Community Social Work A model of social work that describes a team approach to individual and collective issues within a defined community, conducted through early-intervention, preventative and relationship-based approaches.

Critical pedagogy A philosophy of education and social movement that contends that social justice and democracy are facilitated through teaching and learning. Theory developed by Gramsci and Freire (1921–97). See also Pedagogy.

Critical social work The application to social work of theory that addresses social injustices and does not focus on individual issues.

Generalism/ generalist approach The ability to do social work across traditional professional boundaries or specialisms in order to find solutions to problematic issues encountered by service users. Although confused often with generic practice, generalist approaches can be embodied within specialist settings through agreement, and are particularly appropriate in rural locations where specialised resources might not be available.

Generic social work A social work service delivered by the same worker (or team) regardless of need categorisation (child, adult, disability and so on). Specialisation of social work service delivery is now the organisational norm – with models that vary widely between authorities and agencies. The proponents of genericism argue that it allows for the development of skills and knowledge required for effective work in complex settings; its critics suggest that signposting, handovers, duplication and confusion are all associated with specialisation.

Hegemony As an idea developed by Gramsci, this describes the cultural control of society by its dominant class through the use of systems, including press, TV and marketing media, that effectively determine how and what the majority of people think, allowing for rule by consensus.

Homeworking   The practice of working from home using digital technology rather than being office based. Hybrid working now commonplace in social work practice – particularly since the COVID-19 pandemic.

Hot-desking   Sharing offices with others to extent that personal office space not available and there are fewer desks than staff – associated with hybrid working.

Hybrid working   The practice of working from home some of the time and using an office base at others. Proportions on either side vary.

Intersectionality   Describes the interconnected nature of social categorisations such as race, class and gender and how they are experienced by individuals as discriminatory and oppressive.

Managerialist/ Managerialism   This has become a pejorative term used by critics of the style of management that became common in public sector organisations from the 1990s onwards. Based on US neoliberal market-based approaches that emphasised tight financial control, eligibility criteria and prescribed services, allowing little room for professional discretion or autonomy. Associated with New Public Management.

Neoliberal/ Neoliberalism   The belief that free markets in which individuals serve their own material interests, provide the best means for satisfying human aspirations. Its adherents believe that markets are to be preferred over state and political control which are at best inefficient and at worst threats to freedom (Crouch, 2011). In the 19th century such ideas were called 'laissez-fair' and in the US they are known as neo-conservative.

New Public Management   The application of private sector business models to public sector organisations, emphasising the (contested) virtues of effectiveness and efficiency – replacing the traditional public sector focus on social and cultural outcomes and benefits.

Patriarchy   A social system where men enjoy a disproportionately large share of social, economic and religious power, and inheritance passes down the male line.

Pedagogy   The study of the methods and activities of teaching. See also critical pedagogy.

Postcolonialism   The study of the effects of colonialism on cultures and societies: how European nations conquered, exploited and controlled African and other cultures, how they resisted, and how these factors impact on social relations in contemporary society.

Quantitative/   Research terms that describe the origins of
Qualitative   data. Quantitative tends to have numerical significance and is characterised by sets of comparative figures from information gathered and analysed. Qualitative data is based on people's perceptions and opinions, often in small samples but rich in detail and nuance. See also Action Research.

Radical social   Social work practice that seeks to improve
work   the lives of individuals and families, but also strives for structural change through locating and understanding the roots of social problems and poverty.

Relationship-   Based on the premise that the core of good
based/Relational   social work involves human relationships that
social work   are non-blaming, optimistic and hopeful, open and honest, and empathetic.

Third sector   The part of the economy comprising non-governmental and non-profit making organisations and associations, including charities, voluntary groups and co-operatives.

Welfare State   'The complex of social policies and programs that distribute economic resources disproportionally to a nation's vulnerable populations ... (including) progressive taxes, cash and near cash assistance, publicly funded services such as health care, public programs that guarantee economic security, and government programs to ensure social inclusion and economic capability.' (Brady, 2009:7). Welfare states vary in emphasis: Esping-Anderson (1990) suggests three types: the 'liberal' where state provision is modest such as the US, Canada and Australia and increasingly the UK; the 'corporatist' where state provision is shaped by the values of the Church such as France, Germany and Italy in Europe; and the 'social democratic' where state provision is at its most extensive and where equality is more pronounced, such as the Scandinavian countries of Sweden and Norway.

Acknowledgements

This book has been inspired by all the social work practitioners I have met over the years whose earnest desire was to help improve the lives of both individual service users and the communities where they lived. That process is a two-way one, and like many of these people whose work I have admired, my own practice was enhanced by partnerships and engagement with those who I was there to support. Special thanks to Jane Pye for the chapter she has contributed – the latest of several amazing and productive collaborations over recent years. The efforts, artistry and creativity of Fife Council's community social work team colleagues and their senior managers, especially Kathy Henwood (now in Edinburgh City Council), inspired this book. In no particular order (And hoping no one is missed!), others who helped and gave of their time to share ideas and engage in discussion and reflection include: Cerian Twinberrow of Social Care Wales; Kerry Musselbrook of the Institute for Research and Innovation in Social Services (Iriss); Nick Kempe and colleagues on the Common Weal Care Reform Working Group; Stephen Smellie, Kate Ramsden and colleagues on the UNISON Scotland Social Work Issues Group; Alison Bavidge and her team at the Scottish Association of Social Work (SASW); Vita Snowden, Chair of the British Association of Social Work (BASW) Community Social Work Special Interest Group; Fergal O'Brien of the Southern Trust Northern Ireland; Mandy Cowden of the Northern Ireland Social Services Council; and Ben Farrugia and staff at Social Work Scotland. The chapters with practice examples were hugely assisted by the staff concerned: Karen Pedder, Anne Fitzpatrick and Molly Crombie (Fife); Becs Phillips and Gary James (Carmarthenshire); Roisin Ferry and Grainne McAnee (Derry); Sam Jones and Alison Lawson-Jones (Torfaen); and Chris Kidd (Wiltshire).

Introduction

The origins and purpose of this book

This book has been almost 50 years in the making – back to the earliest days of my career, when I was introduced to the notion that community was central to social work. In 1975, still young and impressionable, I started a three-year social work course, from which I qualified in the summer of 1978. Those years were significant, and it is no coincidence that they took place in Edinburgh's Moray House College School of Community Studies. At that time, the student social workers and community workers who were working towards professional qualification studied together for much of the time – only going their separate ways for the more specialised aspects of learning towards the end of their time at Moray House. Community was an important concept drummed into us from the outset – along with some dynamic groupwork ideas that, it must be said, were controversial at the time but that I survived anyway though mostly forgot afterwards. The community ideas, however, left a lasting impression, even if I entered social work in Glasgow after that as no evangelist of community social work (CSW) – such an orientation was simply taken for granted in those early years following implementation of the Scottish legislation (the Social Work Scotland Act 1968) that carried such a notion at its heart. I was, however, committed to the public sector as the place I wanted to practise. This, I believed, was where the real work took place and where collective solutions might be argued for and found. That was still with me almost 40 years later when I retired as a children and family team manager not too far from where I started in the West of Scotland.

A few years after I qualified and started serious social work practice in Glasgow, the Barclay Report brought ideas about CSW into the centre of social work thinking, but did it or had it come too late? Anyway, as experienced by almost all my colleagues, things began to change as we got into the 1990s and we were asked to care-manage adults and focus on risk with children and their families. That took us down bumpy roads, leading in various directions but certainly away from the hearts of the communities we were serving. By that time, I was working in a remote rural setting and, for a while at least, left (and trusted) to just get on with it in whatever way my job-share partner and I thought best. We inherited a good network of colleagues from other agencies and went out of our way to nurture this to the extent that our 'team' was not other social work staff at all but teachers, community and local hospital nurses, police officers, and others, including especially general practitioners (GPs). We all operated generically in our joint working at local level. What messed that up as far as we were concerned was the top-down 'integration' with health that emerged in the early 2000s and remains a mantra to this day. This brought in protocols and systems that seemed to serve the needs of faraway centres rather than our communities. At the same time as all this was happening, colleagues elsewhere were corralled into specialist teams led by siloed managers who had few dealings with one another; generic management in our (by now) reorganised and much smaller local authority was in the hands of very few people. Our notions of generic practice became alien to many, though we tried to celebrate them as a rural practice that suited the needs of where we worked.

Anyway, I became disenchanted with all the contradictions and tensions and finished my formal social work career with several years as a children and family team manager in a post-industrial and left-behind coastal setting in Ayrshire, arguing daily for an orientation that focused on community strengths and weaknesses rather than simply on individual deficits as demonstrated through child safeguarding concerns. By then, 'community' as a focus of social work practice was usually regarded as something we used to do, and while we might have fond memories if we were old enough to remember, there were a pile of report requests and urgent referrals requiring attention, and they were the priority today – and indeed every day – I vented my own frustrations in two books about what social work should, I thought, be like, both of which are foundations of this current work, containing elements of community orientation and practice held and refined since my Moray House days (Turbett, 2010, 2014). After retiring from full-time social work employment and on the back of occasional requests for follow-up presentations and written articles, I began looking in more depth at where it had all gone wrong and how social work might be regenerated. Short papers around these ideas (Turbett, 2018b, 2020, 2021a) and work with Common Weal Scotland colleagues in the Care Reform Working Group have led to this book – via a truly inspiring initiative in Fife, Scotland (of which more later).

The purpose of this book is to set out the reasoning for and context of CSW and then describe in practical terms how it might be put into practice. I am conscious that the subject has received little attention in the literature since the demise of the National Institute of Social Work (NISW) in 2003. Three UK books devoted to the subject have made noteworthy contributions (see Pierson, 2008; Stepney and Popple, 2008; Teater and Baldwin, 2012). However, it is a sign of the times in which they were written that none were able to cite working examples of local authority teams adopting CSW approaches – a difference from the NISW-inspired publications that emerged in the 1980s.

As is explained in detail in the chapters to follow, a central argument of this book is that CSW is not a task that should be relegated to the third sector; rather, the change in practice orientation that is described should be central to mainstream social work service delivery by the public bodies charged with that task – local authorities in England, Scotland and Wales, and (as things stand) health trusts in Northern Ireland. This is therefore a book of principal interest to a UK readership, though I am aware from past study of rural social work internationally how significant the issues discussed are to a North American (including Canadian) and Australasian settler-colonial audience. I am conscious that community forms the basis of social work in the Global South, incorporating ideas ranging from those of Paulo Freire (discussed in Chapter 2) to *Ubuntu* – the African concept that humanness arises from our connection with others, which has been developed into a uniquely postcolonial social work practice that has elements we should recognise in CSW

(Mayaka et al, 2023). However, to describe such practice in full would go beyond the aim of this book, the purpose of which is to provide a guide for the establishment of CSW practice in the mainstream of UK social work.

The US social work writer Hardcastle traces the changes that have taken place in US social work that are also evident in the UK:

> Social work as a profession exists in and reflects the larger society. The decay of social work's social skills and commitment has accompanied the erosion of community spirit and social commitment in the United States. It is reflective of the 'me-ism', the libertarian, self-centred philosophy currently rampant, and the social isolation and fragmentation of contemporary America ... community as a basis of identification has become exclusionary rather than inclusionary. (Hardcastle et al, 2011: 10–11)

Social work should be a profession concerned with issues (poverty, exclusion, social isolation and so on) that are collectively as well as individually experienced, and this community development role, considered essential if it is to meet its transformative potential, is the subject of the following chapters.

Some definitions

Given the use of the word 'community' and the term 'community social work' throughout this book, the reader will be saved confusion if these terms are examined in the context of social work practice and some consensus offered about their meaning. These will then be used throughout the chapters that follow and appear in the book's glossary.

'Community' and 'neighbourhood' are often used interchangeably, so at the outset, differences between them must be clarified so that when they are used in the text, that difference is understood. Both also overlap with 'society' (which in turn overlaps with 'state'), adding further to the confusion. Society as a concept is interpreted widely, but the meaning used summarises the shared beliefs, culture and acceptance through laws and rules of conduct that aspire to provide order, stability and identity, usually to a nation (definition adapted from the Concise Oxford Dictionary). Within an autocratic society, there might be attempts to enforce a set of beliefs based on a single culture, but in the societies under discussion here, there is a widespread acceptance of cultural differences based on tradition, religious belief and other practices and backgrounds, implying a general acceptance of diversity even though struggles to gain equality by minority groups and people not of White British origin continue.

Beneath the concept of society lies the Italian Marxist philosopher Gramsci's notion of 'civil society'; this sits alongside his use of the term 'hegemony', that is, the process by which the dominant ruling class perpetuate their power and authority not just through coercion but through gaining popular acceptance of their values and views of the world through their control of the media and other means by which ideas are shared. While society is an intangible concept, the parallel concept of 'state' has a clearer (if often contested) definition, meaning the public institutions that provide government and security. All these explanations contain complexities that, as Gramsci (1982) described, disguise class differences, inequality and oppression to the extent that a national identity, purpose and commonly accepted set of values remain an ideal and aspiration of most, if not all, societies.

Pierson (2008) offers a useful social-work-orientated discussion of the concepts of community and neighbourhood, as well as their origins: while 'community' as a term has complicated and varied meanings, 'neighbourhood' has emerged as more clearly defined in the sense of a small area around an individual's place of residence where social relations might be based on face-to-face contact even if relations are not close. Government and policy-making bodies might regard a neighbourhood as a larger area; in recent times, the concept of the '15-minute neighbourhood' (sometimes '20-minute neighbourhood'), where amenities can be accessed by foot or cycle within 15 (20) minutes, has become popular with town planners (Smart Transport, 2023). The 15-minute concept has grown in stature since the COVID-19 pandemic, where during lockdown (as discussed in Chapter 1), communities were forced to support themselves as normal access to services became problematic, especially for the vulnerable.

If neighbourhood is defined geographically, what about 'community'? For many people, their community is also defined in physical terms. Pierson (2008) suggests that the term emerged in opposition to the nebulous concept of society, meaning something much warmer that involved a high degree of identification and connection. This idea was carried into post-war sociological studies of working-class areas, sometimes based on a few large manufacturers or labour-intensive employment (like deep coal mining), which were found to be homogeneous in ethnic and class terms. Such places were characterised by commonly shared beliefs and behaviours, extending into faith, leisure activity, world views and voting patterns. The 1980s saw the destruction of many such communities through deindustrialisation and population change, leading inevitably to a necessary redefinition based on more than just neighbourhood and common identity. Community was now regarded as something very different, where it could and should not be assumed that a single geographical space contained a dominant set of values, beliefs and other definitions that might have both positive and negative connotations. Instead, it was accepted that any locality might host various communities based around faith, ethnicity, language, culture and identification arising from disability, sexual orientation and age. Postmodern thinking added to the traditional notion of community by adding that social individualism had become so embedded that the idea of a community was dated and based on outmoded concepts of social connection. The decline of volunteering was seen as a sign of this trend. Communities of interest, others suggested more persuasively perhaps, could be experienced across spaces far apart through common identities, especially, we might now argue, in the age of digital communication. While these postmodern critiques were spanners in the works of social planners and policy makers, the idea that community had become so nebulous as to be redundant as a concept never took complete hold. Communities at the locality level still contain centres in which people shop, meet, get educated and engage in all sorts of activities. As already said, and to be explored in more detail later, COVID-19 brought all this into sharp relief and clarified matters for some, including myself.

Shaw (2011 [2008]: 305) discusses the concept of the 'contrived community': the manner in which community is romanticised and imbued with character in hindsight that might have been absent as lived experience at the time. Thus, while the mining communities that were vigorously defended during the 1984–85 Miners' Strike were close and connected by shared work experience, this was underpinned by hardship and periods of great poverty, so that membership might have been given up at a stroke if their inhabitants had any real choice. Therefore, deprivation in an age of austerity can lend itself to a negative identity in order to attract scarce targeted funding for projects and initiatives. For Shaw, the concept of community is sometimes constructed to serve the interests of policy makers who like to see the object of their interventions as natural and harmonious entities rather than ones contrived by planners and faceless bureaucracies.

A definition of CSW is now needed to bring all this back to the premise of the book. As will be described in Chapter 1, CSW reached its zenith in the 1980s, just as the traditional working-class communities, where such social problems as poverty and deprivation had always been most concentrated, were suffering a process of dismembering. The CSW projects and initiatives at that time were focused on clearly defined localities. These changes were not to lead to CSW's demise – in fact, it was arguably more needed that ever in those years – but other factors were at work that led to that end, as we shall see. However, the model of CSW as a bottom-up entity based on local ownership and direction had been established, at least as an ideal, and formed the basis of a modern definition that this book will take forward, which can be summarised as follows:

- a de-individualisation of social work's approach to commonly experienced social problems and issues;
- relationship-based approaches that seek to prevent the escalation of issues, using the skills that social workers learn through professional education and training;
- upstream approaches to identifying and tackling these common problems and their individual manifestations through early identification and mutually agreed solutions;
- the use of a variety of approaches, including groupwork, activity-based programmes and social action;

- having roots in the communities served, drawing strength and purpose from community networks (including with other agencies), activists and members;
- created through bottom-up activity rather than top-down prescription, and, as such, requiring supportive and enabling managers at all levels, policy makers, and politicians; and
- delivered through mainstream services, not as peripheral and farmed-out activities to the third (voluntary) sector.

It is important from this early stage to delineate the model described here, which is consistent with the descriptions of CSW from the 1970s–90s period, from use of the term that has arisen since. Obviously, there is no copyright or precise dictionary definition – CSW is referenced in the *Oxford Dictionary of Social Work and Social Care* (Harris and White, 2018), but under the Barclay Report of 1982 (Barclay, 1982; see also Chapter 1), as a historical matter rather than of relevance to contemporary practice. There is confusion with what I describe in Chapter 2 of this book as a 'community orientation': awareness of context and promotion and use of networks and other methods that might also be found in CSW practice. However, these alone, laudable though they are in comparison with the centralised and individual risk-averse practice often found today in many statutory settings, do not make for CSW, as they are still focused on individual deficits. Smale et al (1988) felt it necessary to explore this theme and outline what CSW was *not*:

- The practice of a community social worker;
- The odd project/group/volunteer tacked on to a case orientated team;
- Community work;
- Just about informal care networks;
- Solely about a shift in the balance of provision between local authority services and the voluntary sector – though partnership in joint planning is crucial. (Smale et al, 1988: 54)

This list has stood the test of time. All its components are worthy in themselves and, with others that will be identified later in the book, should be considered to formulate what will be described as community-orientated practice rather than CSW. This is important to emphasise because it seems to the author that there is confusion in at least one recent example of literature: Teater and Baldwin (2012). Forde and Lynch (2015) take a rather different approach to the idea of CSW and criticise it as a concept for being individualistic in its approach, being apolitical and lacking clarity about its nature and focus. Their book discusses positively the idea of community development in social work, an idea that in its reality rather than as a theoretical notion, I prefer to consider as community-orientated practice.

Finding your way around the book

Chapter 1 looks at some history of CSW, from its origins in plans for the welfare state during the Second World War to its practice demise in the 1990s and persistence as an important strand of radical social work ideology. This draws upon reports of practice from the 1970s–90s period, the author's own writings and the more contemporary work of commentators like Stepney and Popple (2008). An examination is given of two examples of CSW teams from the 1980s, which are of more than historical interest, as they offer lessons of value today. The chapter examines the legislation of the 1960s that embodied notions of community as central to social services and the Barclay Report of 1982, where the idea was put up as a model for the future of social work in England. The reasons for the demise of CSW towards the end of the 20th century are outlined, and critical commentary is offered. The chapter also addresses the socio-economic context of social work in the UK today and its evolution. It examines social work's role through the 2020–21 period of COVID-19 and how communities were mobilised to provide support to their members. In this context, a critique is offered of the way community action and voluntary effort can be used to reduce the scope of publicly provided services; this points towards an emphasis throughout the book that CSW should not be consigned to the third sector (I use this description rather than 'non-governmental organisations' [NGOs], as it is more widely used and understood in the UK context).

Chapter 2 focuses on the subject, raised earlier, of 'community orientation'. It looks at its history and description in the literature as a concept and describes how it might be introduced consciously into mainstream practice. This will suggest reasons why it might be overlooked in current service delivery models and how a team culture can be created that puts community at the front and centre of practice. It will address the concerns raised earlier that contemporary social work practice is often delivered from inaccessible centralised office buildings where hot-desking and enforced homeworking militate against team building and cooperation.

Drawing on both old and more contemporary literature, Chapter 3 will look at the model of CSW as a modern concept worthy of investment and priority. It describes how the basics of community development theory can be applied to social work delivered on a preventative and supportive basis where people live and gather (and describes 'community work' so that differences are clear). It will employ the oft-used metaphor that if you help to stop people falling into the river, they will not need to be rescued from drowning downstream. The chapter considers a model of transition from traditional to CSW-based practice and suggests that while this might seem a luxury during a time of (never-ending) austerity, the actuality is that public bodies cannot afford *not* to incorporate such models given the rising social and financial cost of focusing their activities downstream. That cost is also resulting in a recruitment and retention crisis as workers become ever-more dissatisfied with the tasks they are expected to perform. CSW approaches, it is argued, should utilise the professional skills of trained social workers and not rely upon poorly paid workers employed by insecurely funded third sector organisations.

To provide some background context for Chapters 5 to 8, Chapter 4 will summarise the legislative and policy drivers that might assist the process of funding and promoting CSW initiatives. This summary will inevitably date quickly but exemplifies opportunities that might be available in each of the four administrations, as well as some legal background.

Chapters 5, 6, 7 and 8 examine current or very recent examples of CSW practice in, respectively, England, Wales, Scotland and Northern Ireland. Where possible, these accounts will include the voices of service users as well as the staff involved. I have quite deliberately chosen to showcase examples from the local authority sector in order to underline one of the main messages of the book: that mainstream local authority social work is in need of transformation and that CSW offers a way forward. This has presented issues: it would have been fairly straightforward to find examples of great innovative CSW from the third sector, but this would have missed the point being made. This may disappoint some readers who might know of examples that better exemplify CSW than some of the ones chosen here. However, for reasons outlined already, I have decided to use some bold examples from workers trying to make a difference in very different statutory settings across the UK. Chapter 9 follows from these four chapters and draws conclusions, commonalities, learning and lessons from the examples of practice offered.

Any book about communities and their importance for social work has to consider the impact of climate change and the place of social work in addressing all the issues this brings. CSW is, Chapter 10 argues, well placed to both build resilience in places that are vulnerable and intervene where disaster has occurred.

Chapter 11, written by guest contributor Jane Pye of the University of Lancaster, takes a look at social work education. As well as a consideration of possibilities and barriers to instilling community social work in undergraduate professional training, Jane will also look at postgraduate possibilities.

Chapter 12 concludes the book with a summary chapter drawing conclusions concerning the future of CSW in the UK. It also translates previous material in the book into a practical guide for practitioners, managers and community activists, both on community orientation and on suggested steps for the establishment of a CSW team. This is presented in the form of tables that summarise the content of previous chapters.

The book's purpose

This is not the first attempt at offering a handbook on CSW: *A Community Social Worker's Handbook* by Roger Hadley and colleagues appeared in 1987 (Hadley et al, 1987) – too late, as it turned out, to seriously influence trends that were to reach fruition in the 1990s with the onset of business models and the diminution of social work's importance (issues addressed in Chapter 1). We live with that legacy today, with, many of us would contend, attendant dissatisfaction by practitioners with much of what they are asked to do in statutory settings. This is accompanied with suspicion by the public about the profession based on the experiences and failures of its public protection role, much of which has oppressive aspects. Social work has lost its way and, like a broken limb, needs a reset if we are to return to a functioning profession that fulfils its potential and promise.

This is a book about the possible rather than some kind of unattainable ideal based on a golden age of social work long before most current workers came into practice. That golden age never existed anyway. The book is not arrogantly arguing that effective social work absolutely has to be based around notions of community-based practice; good social work is possible in any setting, including, if discretion is exercised effectively, in the most constrained and proceduralised care management settings. Social work is about seeing people for who they are, and its possibilities in contemporary settings are demonstrated by the authors of the wonderful text *Social Work, Cats and Rocket Science* (James et al, 2020). They are absolutely right when they criticise colleagues who 'hide behind concepts and defences' and argue that 'if you think the key decision … is allocation of funding or bestowing of services via a care plan, then you are just focusing on buying stuff' (James et al, 2020: 136). Social work is more creative than that, involving both artistry and knowledge based on science, and it is believed that preventative relationship-based CSW offers opportunities from which everyone can benefit – in effect, a rescue plan from the constraints and dilemmas of the kind of practice that has become the norm since the 1990s.

There has been a recent rebirth of interest in bringing community back into social work, as evidenced in several chapters of this book. It is hoped that the content builds on this by providing some history, background and context, as well as theory and practical advice. If it succeeds, it will contribute to the serious rediscovery and recognition of CSW's place as a supportive and relationship-based model that realistically faces up to all the problems and issues with social work delivery at the present time.

1

A history of community social work in the UK

The founding of the welfare state and the growth of state social work

The Second World War was preceded by economic crisis and social dislocation, and by the time it was just a year old in 1940, the government and War Office realised that as it was not going well, incentives were needed to raise morale among the fighting troops and population which could promote more enthusiastic engagement in the war effort. This took several forms, the best known being the plans for social insurance as the foundation of a welfare state – the Beveridge Report that was published in 1942. This was aimed directly at tackling the 'Five Giants' – want, disease, ignorance squalor and idleness – that had stalked the land through the 1930s (Beveridge, 1943). By the time of the report's publication, the systematic education of the troops had already commenced through a reinvigorated Army Education Service and briefings discussed on a weekly basis with all military units not in actual combat, drawn up by the Army Bureau of Current Affairs and led by unit officers. These had two purposes: first, to inform about the progress of the war; and, second, to encourage discussion about the shape of post-war Britain and the issues it might face. While elements of these programmes were clearly aimed at defending the status quo, much of the content was framed by anti-fascist socialists and communists who had been recruited into the Army Education Service. These included content on such topics as social security, youth services and community centres in (to quote Beveridge) the 'New Britain' that would follow military victory (Bennett, 1945; Downs, 1945). The pamphlet that followed the publication of the Beveridge Report in 1942 was banned and pulped on the orders of Prime Minister Churchill, who was unhappy with some of the proposals; it was only published in amended form the following year with an accompanying cautionary note from Churchill. An official paper during this period on community planning looked at the shape of communities, the need for amenities like 'community centres' in the new estates that would be required to solve the housing crisis and how citizenship and participation might be encouraged and nurtured (Stephenson and Stephenson 1942). The aim was clearly to give the fighting troops and overworked war industry and food producers something to fight and work for, and the message was not lost: the 1945 general election saw the Labour Party, who were committed to the implementation of the Beveridge Report and creating a welfare state, win a landslide victory. The reference here to discussion about community centres (that is, buildings) during this period is intentional: this community development theme is overlooked in the literature otherwise quoted favourably in this book (see, for example, Craig et al, 2011; Ledwith, 2020) but regained significance during the COVID-19 pandemic through the use of 'community hubs' (discussed later in this chapter) – with more than an echo here of wartime experience and aspiration.

The implementation of Beveridge's report saw the establishment within local authorities throughout the UK of the three bodies that were to become the hosts of social work services run by the state: children's, welfare and mental health departments (probation services were run by the central government and, with the exception of Scotland, remain organised this way until the present day). The years that followed saw debate among social work's leaders and commentators of what the values and identity of the new profession should be. Two strands emerged: on the one hand, the influential pioneer Eileen Younghusband believed that social work needed a social action emphasis to address social problems experienced through poverty and other disadvantage; on the other, the Freudian psychodynamic tradition's proponents believed that the focus should be on personality. Younghusband's views were reflected in her 1947 report into the social work profession and its place in the UK. While this sought to put social work on the map in the immediate aftermath of war, its very broad definition of what social workers do (some of which we would ascribe to other professions today) talked of three settings: casework, groupwork and community organisation (Younghusband, 1947). Another early post-war definition of social work by the British Federation of Social Workers reflected these tensions within a statement that offered no hint of the public protection and safeguarding role that seems to have overtaken statutory social work in recent years:

> A professional social worker is one who is employed to provide some social service for individuals or groups of individuals. The aim of the service should be to work in co-operation with the individual in such a way that his or her potentialities are given the fullest possible scope in relation to the community of which he or she is a member. (Quoted in Simey, 1947: 10)

In social work casework (delivered through case management), the approach to the client's issues was neatly summarised by Helen Perlman's (1957) 'four P's': the problem, the person, the place and the process. It should be noted here that 'place' refers to the agency where the worker is located, not the community context of the client. Similarly, Florence Hollis (1964) defined casework as a method of helping an individual find solutions to problems of social adjustment. The individualisation involved in such interactions was deliberate: casework theory holds that as individuals have different personalities based on their own history, they require a unique and personal service. Perlman's and Hollis's works were (with others of the same genre) given reverence and primacy on social work courses in that era, though alongside other theory that considered the individual's interaction with the social environment without suggesting challenge (the systems theory of Pincus and Minahan [1973] was a popular example). Whether there really was a 'psychiatric deluge' within social work at this time is debatable (Cree, 1995). Certainly, Younghusband, whose book *Social Work and Social Change* (Younghusband, 1964) was the first publication of the National Institute for Social Work (NISW), drew on the example of the early 19th-century pioneers of social work in the UK (Charles Booth, the Webbs and others) to further her argument that social workers needed to focus on the individual *and* their social environment if unwanted, intrusive and ineffective interventions were to be avoided – something well worth reminding ourselves of today. She was also clear that this was all underwritten by the importance of relationships.

The social action school was very influential in the growth of social work in the UK in the post-war period, to the extent of shaping the legislation that created social services departments in England and Wales and social work departments in Scotland in the 1960s. This was helped along by the influential sociologist and social commentator Barbara Wootton, who, in 1959, claimed that social work 'confused economic difficulties with personal failure or misconduct' (quoted in Langan, 2011: 161). The 359-page 1959 report of a government working party into the role of social workers across the UK, chaired by Eileen Younghusband, suggested a generic qualification for social workers, 85 per cent of whom had little or no training, and a focus on 'the social and personal needs of the family, rather than on a particular aspect of the problem' (Ministry of Health, Department of Health for Scotland, 1959: 9). It further suggested that there should be 'A new emphasis on the contribution social workers can make to the prevention as well as the alleviation of the social problems of individuals and families' (Ministry of Health, Department of Health for Scotland, 1959: 152). A key factor in this focus was the growing recognition that despite rising standards of living in a booming economy, poverty and deprivation were lingering as issues, especially in parts of the country where they had long existed: social workers were busy picking up the pieces in these forgotten corners of the big cities and deindustrialised areas of the UK (Ferguson and Woodward, 2009). The book *The Client Speaks* (Mayer and Timms, 1970) vividly described the experiences of working-class people who were in receipt of social work interventions. While it is imbued with casework concepts of 'treatment', it honestly suggests that individuals and their families struggling with poverty and disadvantage were only likely to have their needs met by material assistance; anything else was like 'offering clothes to a drowning man' (Mayer and Timms, 1970: 140).

In England and Wales, the framework for bringing together the various strands of post-war social work delivery into a single service delivered by local authorities was established in the Seebohm Report of 1968. Its 370 pages were forward-thinking, and some of its findings have not dated over the years since, even if they might have been forgotten. Throughout, the personal issues that might require an individual or family to seek or require social work support were placed within the context of their social situation and economic circumstances:

> Our emphasis on the importance of the community does not stem from a belief that the small, closely-knit rural community of the past could be reproduced in the urban society of today and of the future. Our interest in the community is not nostalgic in origin, but based on the practical grounds that the community is both the provider as well as the recipient of social services, and that orientation to the community is vital if the services are to be directed to individuals, families and groups within the context of their social relations with others. (UK Government, 1968: 147)

Having heard evidence and considered arguments in favour of centralisation, Seebohm was also clear that the proper place for social services was within local authorities. The role of voluntary organisations was explored, and problems that have emerged in our own times (the way in which third sector organisations, sometimes funded directly by government, have assumed basic welfare provision roles) were considered: 'voluntary organisations may act as direct agents of the local authority in providing particular services, though such arrangements can present problems both to the local authority and to the voluntary organisation which may be prevented from fulfilling its critical and pioneer role' (UK Government, 1968: 152). In Scotland, similar trends emerged in efforts to modernise and reshape social work. The 1966 government white paper *Social Work in the Community* that followed the publication of the 1964 Kilbrandon Report had notions of community at its heart:

> Whatever their immediate disability or difficulty, people can seldom overcome it by personal efforts alone. The majority of people tackle it in cooperation with, and with the support of, their family and community. But there is a minority who need help of the kind that social services can give to establish and strengthen the personal and social relationships which can provide this co-operation and support. (Scottish Education Department, Scottish Home and Health Department, 1966: 3)

It went on to describe the role of social work, which, in conjunction with other agencies, would engage with wider issues affecting local communities:

> To take the community first, it seems clear that physical environment affects social development and behaviour. ... Physical planning and change involve social factors, which in the past have not always been taken fully into account. ... The creation of a new social work department in touch with all the problems of an area will change this situation. (Scottish Education Department, Scottish Home and Health Department, 1966: 5)

The report's final words on its aspiration for the new social work departments echo down the years in their lost significance:

> It is important to recognise, however, that the new organisation, however well it may be conceived and designed, can do no more than set the stage. Its success will depend on the extent to which all the professional workers concerned can co-operate with each other and can enlist the whole resources of the community. The new organisation will realise its potential only as that co-operation and community

action extend and become fully effective. (Scottish Education Department, Scottish Home and Health Department, 1966: 21)

An important factor here was the local authority duty in Scotland to 'promote social welfare' in terms of Section 12 of the Social Work (Scotland) Act 1968 that followed. This was clearly intended to be taken seriously, as guidance issued by the Social Work Services Group (the government agency in Scotland responsible for providing guidance and direction to local authorities) was clear:

> Social workers should be attentive to events and developments within the communities they serve, anticipating needs that are likely to arise. ... The workload of local authority social work teams should be planned to include activity designed to explore and monitor situations and developments within communities they serve with a view to anticipating need and planning ahead for the provision to meet it. ... Social workers should be attentive to the plans and activities of agencies – their own and any others … it might involve, for example, direct negotiation, enabling people in the community to exercise direct influence, and/or referring information to senior management level for action. (Quoted in Turbett, 2018b: 7)

It should be noted that the duty to promote social welfare did not find its way into the Local Authority Social Services Act 1970 that followed the Seebohm Report in England. Although this had been sought by the social work lobby, it was omitted as a compromise to the medical officers of health lobby who saw this as a diminution in their role (Prynn and Rappaport, 2009).

The post-war development of services in Northern Ireland largely reflected the changes in the rest of the UK, but commensurate with the wish of its devolved administration to prove its services superior to those south of the border – what has been described as 'differential universality' – a welfare state with a unionist flavour was created (Heenan and Birrell, 2011: 17). Against a background of endemic discrimination against the nationalist population and The Troubles that emerged out of the Civil Rights Movement of 1968, self-government in Northern Ireland was prorogued and Direct Rule from Westminster introduced in 1972. This is not the place to describe the complexities and consequences of this, but a significant direction was taken with the rather pragmatic 1972 legislation that bypassed problematic issues in local government by integrating health and social services into health and social services boards. These survive to this day in the form of the five health and social care trusts.

The 1970s to the 1990s: the rise and fall of social work

The new social services and social work departments were set up at a time of great hope for social work. Professional training had expanded to the extent that the new departments were staffed by increasing numbers of qualified staff, displacing the experienced but often unqualified staff who had provided the backbone of the old departments. This new generation brought hope and a determination to improve services (Rogowski, 2020). Ideas of radical social work were widely read even if not often carried into the reality of workplaces (Bailey and Brake, 1975; Corrigan and Leonard, 1978; Turbett, 2014). How to bring social work closer to communities was much discussed at a time when offices offering a generic service were in the neighbourhoods they served. The Barclay Report of 1982, a wide-ranging committee review whose aim was to provide an informed basis for taking forward the profession in England, concluded that community social work (CSW) offered a strong model (Barclay, 1982). This was based on the idea that social work should focus on two areas: counselling (that is, social casework) and social planning (what we would now term the 'co-design' of services alongside neighbourhood members in the context of prevention and community development). CSW delivery models might vary from neighbourhood 'patch' teams to social workers located in schools, hospitals or general practitioner (GP) practices. This had some support within the profession, but a minority report by sociologist Robert Pinker (appearing as an appendix to the main report) argued that the focus should be on individuals and skills in social casework, which were proven in practice and could be built upon with no great changes necessary. This echoed a previous right-wing-inspired text of the same era which suggested that training should concentrate on tried-and-tested methods like behavioural approaches (Brewer and Lait, 1980). From the left wing of social work, there were warnings, relevant today, that Barclay's vision could be used to reduce public services and place reliance on local volunteers and the private sector (Beresford and Croft, 1984). However, as the years went by, it was clear that Pinker's arguments found more favour with the Tory government and senior social services managers, and there was no major roll-out of CSW (Harris, 2008). By the time of Barclay's publication, social work had passed its period of ascendancy: public services were subject to regular rounds of budget cuts following the financial crisis invoked by a sudden increase in oil prices in 1973 and then subject to political disfavour with the election of a Tory government led by the monetarist Margaret Thatcher in 1979. This was not a good time for innovation requiring serious investment.

Inspired by Barclay, several CSW initiatives did emerge across the UK in the 1980s. These were usually very localised in nature and typically involved enthusiastic local managers and staff cooperating with community activists to create the kind of bottom-up service consistent with the definition of CSW outlined in the Introduction to this book. The NISW, founded in 1963 with independent funding to promote social work throughout the UK and later grant-funded by government, did much to promote CSW at this time – a reflection of the enthusiasm of some of their key staff, such as Gerald Smale and Graham Tuson. Thanks to their publication output and the work of other CSW adherents, we have several examples that can be reviewed today, two of which will be briefly showcased here. It must be explained that this is not a random selection: those chosen represent examples from local authorities and not from the many worthy voluntary sector initiatives. Given the climate and context explained earlier, those cited here were all brave attempts to carry through the promise of Barclay to transform local-authority-provided social work services – all foundered for reasons that will be explained.

Historical Example 1: Whitehill Patch Team, Hamilton, Strathclyde Region, Scotland, 1983–85

The Hamilton example, written up by one of its social workers, Pam Green, was featured in Smale and Bennett (1989). The patch team was formed from four interested social workers from the area team (at that time, offering a generic service) serving the much larger town in which this clearly defined small area of council housing (population 3,500) was located. Prior research based on local statistics suggested that there was an over-preponderance of statutory referrals, alongside a dearth of self-referrals. The Whitehill Patch Team initiative sat alongside other less concerted attempts to deliver patch-based services in other parts of the area, resulting in confusion and tension between staff. The Whitehill staff set out to improve accessibility, promote and facilitate community action, and widen service delivery choices. Despite these ambitions and prior discussion involving Glasgow University staff, plans were realised in a piecemeal fashion, and the implications of changes in working practices were not thought through properly. Premises were shared with the tenants association – an arrangement that was unsatisfactory due to its virtual monopoly by social work staff and users. Dedicated community worker membership of the team was never properly realised, but groupwork activities facilitated by the team's own groupworker flourished and resulted in dialogue with and involvement by young people from the area (half the area's population were under 16).

A huge increase in self-referrals took up much social worker time, but the way issues to do with benefits, debt and other practical matters were dealt with was popular in the community. Statutory referrals dropped and social workers increasingly sought informal solutions to issues involving youth crime and even child safeguarding. On one occasion, a reception into care of children during a crisis involving a heavily drinking parent was avoided through mobilising the support of neighbours (challenging some notions of confidentiality).

After less than a year, a social worker was withdrawn to cover shortages elsewhere and because the success of the patch team at reducing statutory referrals suggested, paradoxically, that fewer were needed. Other tensions added to staff demoralisation, and all the remaining three social workers departed for jobs elsewhere, leading to the patch team's reintegration into the main area team after a life of less than two years.

Historical Example 2: Normanton Area Team, Wakefield Metropolitan District Council, West Yorkshire, 1979–80

The Normanton Area Team and its three sub-patch teams were researched and written about in a published NISW book by Hadley and McGrath (1984). Although this does not describe the eventual fate of the team, it does provide an extensive and valuable account of their work and compares it with the traditional approach taken by the neighbouring team in Featherstone, an area with similar demographics.

Normanton's population was about 18,000 at the time, and the social services team had just moved to the area from their centralised base in nearby Pontefract. The new team, Hadley and McGrath note, was an average size for a post-Seebohm area team. The area officer, Mike Cooper, had worked in the community development project (CDP) in Batley and was a keen exponent of CSW. His criticism of traditional methods was based on a belief that 'the client was at once the object and the enemy of the agency' and that services were defensive and deliberately inaccessible to put limits on the workload (Hadley and McGrath, 1984: 35). Through recruitment and dialogue with staff, he set about creating three patches connected to the area team: Altofts, Woodhouse and Castleford Road. Each patch was staffed by two 'neighbourhood workers' – a redesignated social work assistant and senior home help – who worked alongside a 'patch leader' who was a qualified social worker. Most of the neighbourhood workers lived on the patch and were selected because of their local knowledge and networking experience. They were tasked with going out and about in the neighbourhood and bringing any issues they could not solve themselves back to their patch leader.

Each patch staff group was given permission to develop in its own way, and the research showed that three variations emerged based on the interests of and closeness to the community of the workers involved – one patch had a patch leader who was 'client-orientated' (a traditional casework orientation) compared, respectively, to the 'familial' (focused on knowledge of family networks) and 'quasi-community' (focus on community networks) of the other two. However, in broad terms, when compared with the neighbouring Featherstone Area Team, positive outcomes were recorded in the following domains:

- Knowledge: there was evidence that the patch team members were better able to identify those most at risk at an earlier stage than their Featherstone neighbours – 40 per cent of new family or individual referrals were already known to staff.
- Accessibility: informal referrals were some 40 per cent higher in total than those in Featherstone, indicating trust in the team.
- Mobilising resources: the area officer suggested that the broader roles (that is, generalist roles) adopted by team members, their closer interaction with informal support systems, improved collaboration with other agencies and the creation of additional resources had all increased effectiveness.
- Broader roles of staff: all staff were involved in groupwork and community work, as well as traditional casework, and administrative staff were involved in weekly team meetings. However, there was little progress in involving home helps more fully into the patch team, usually through choice.
- Building informal support systems: data could not confirm this, but anecdotal evidence and referrals from neighbours, relatives and friends, as well as ensuing contact, suggest that this was an 'essential precondition for successful collaboration' (Hadley and McGrath, 1984: 255).
- Work with other agencies: the Normanton Area Team established both formal and informal relationships with other agencies and their staff than did the Featherstone Area Team, and these were not dependent upon shared cases.
- Creation of additional resources: the patch teams recruited local volunteers, sponsored groups with mothers, children and young people, started clubs, ran outings, and helped set up community organisations.
- Work satisfaction: this was reported to be at a higher level among ancillary staff, who were asked to participate fully in developing the team's activity. This was considered difficult

to measure for social workers given the very different commitments required.

In general, the researchers considered that the Normanton Area Team had made good progress with implementing a model of CSW but that full autonomy to progress further was beyond the scope of the team and the resources available to its staff and their leaders. In hindsight, it has to be noted that the level of autonomy they did enjoy would have been impossible in the climate of New Public Management (NPM) and centralised control that emerged a few years later.

Social work services from the 1990s to the present day

The blended social work practice that emphasised individual need but largely accepted recognition of the social situation continued into the 1990s. By this time, social work was on the defensive – unfairly mired with accusations of incompetence in the wake of child protection scandals and undervalued by a Tory government looking to cut public spending for ideological reasons (Teater and Baldwin, 2012; Jones, 2014). In the same era, the NHS and Community Care Act 1990 saw social work and social care become subject to markets, business models and the privatisation of services. This was a deliberate right-wing political incursion: the report that preceded it (Griffiths, 1988) used much the same language as Barclay – choice, independence and participation for users and carers (Ferguson and Woodward, 2009) – but, being written by a business rather than social policy expert, led matters in a new direction. The 'care in the community' that the new legislation facilitated was underwritten with business concepts: care management replaced casework, and social workers increasingly became brokers and care managers rather than providers of support for the individuals and families they worked with (Harris, 2003). Practitioner and writer Elaine James and her colleagues (2020: 69) describe how this has resulted in workers and the people they support becoming caught up in 'Serviceland', a place where 'casual dismissal of the small things that define a good life have become the norm, where the protection imperative dominates'. It is worth noting that 'care management' was the term preferred by service user organisations, which considered it derogatory to be considered as 'cases' in the terminology of casework and case management (Harris and White, 2018). In the years since, critics of the introduction of business methods into social work have come to associate care management with proceduralised approaches that have diminished relationship-based social work, and it is in that sense that the term is used throughout this book (see, for example, Harris, 2003; James et al, 2020).

Uniformity and centralised control under managers imbued with the language of NPM replaced any notion of the bottom-up community building of services. This involved: a shift by public sector leaders from involvement in policy making to management; interest in quantifiable performance measurements and appraisal; the breakup of structures into business units purchasing services from one another; market testing and tendering (rather than automatic in-house service provision); an emphasis on cost cutting; output targets rather than input controls; short-term contracts for staff rather than job security; and the use of regulatory mechanisms rather than legislation to ensure quality (McDonald, 2006). While these were general trends in the public sector, within social work, services became increasingly specialised and organisationally fragmented; in fact, organisational change became a feature, as constantly moving senior managers made their mark with seemingly never-ending structural change within their cash-strapped empires. Harris (2003: 76) compares this managerialist process to 'McDonaldisation', the US writer Ritzer's description of the four principles of the fast-food corporation: 'efficiency, predictability, calculability and control through non-human technology'. This analogy was taken further in a researched examination of the practice of care management in the UK, concluding that the construction of service users as business customers was not a credible means to their empowerment (Dustin, 2007). This author also found that the prescriptive practice associated with care management, whether with adults or children, was deskilling for workers in that it removed areas of professional discretion.

Social work experience and knowledge at that level was replaced by skills in NPM; in fact, the important public role that social work and social services directors had enjoyed from the 1970s on was undermined by local government reorganisation in Scotland in the 1990s and England and Wales a few years later (Brodie et al, 2008). Social work's status consequently suffered, and this was to be exaggerated further by the rounds of integration with (a much larger and more powerful) health service that followed from 2000 onwards. Social workers are now likely to have senior managers from outside the profession (including a few examples in Scotland of chief executive officer [CEO] posts being held by accountants), reflecting their NPM rather than social work experience and expertise. All this has been impacted negatively by austerity following the collapse of the banks, their consequent publicly funded bailouts in 2008 and rising demands as inequality increases (Dorling, 2018).

Community development and community work

This chapter is mainly concerned with history, and given the crossovers between CSW, community development and community action, some space is needed to explain the fit (or otherwise) between them. Community work as a profession emerged from under the umbrella of social work in the 1950s and 1960s, and by 1968, it had successfully defined itself enough to prove it required its own professional training (Younghusband, 1968). This freed it from what some saw as domination by social work, as evidenced earlier in this chapter. Community work as an autonomous occupation involving community action reached its peak with the CDPs of the 1970s. These were government-funded local-authority-run projects in run-down areas of Britain; contrary to the intent of funders, workers joined tenants and others in identifying and challenging the impact of structural decline, supporting rent strikes and other acts of resistance. This resulted in eventual withdrawal of funding and the closure of the projects. Banks (2011) describes how the CDPs had moved from attempts at community development (what a group of CDP workers in a 1977 booklet described as 'Gilding the Ghetto' [CDP Inter-Project Editorial Team, 1977]) to community action and conflict with authority, eventually realising that local solutions to economic decline were illusory. This anti-statist radical campaigning aspect to community work in the 1970s did not fit well with the community social work model being promoted by NISW, and such tensions did not help the take-up of CSW ideas when these were posed as liberal and accommodating of the status quo (Craig et al, 2011).

However, the political climate of a Tory government caught up with community work: from the 1980s, community work, usually located within local authorities, became increasingly targeted on less politically challenging areas, such as adult education, youth work, community care, community health and, in recent years, participatory budgeting. While all these contain the potential for community action, as they rest on notions of empowerment of the individual and the community, there are 'ambiguities and contradictions about the values and motives of community programmes ... particularly those sponsored by the state' (Mayo, 2005, quoted in Craig et al, 2011: 14). Perhaps taking a more idealised and generic view of community work and a social work model that could only be found in some individual practice, Stepney and Popple (2008: 113) describe the difference in orientation between it and CSW: 'Community work is concerned with tackling injustice by organising people and promoting policy change at the local level. CSW is concerned with developing more accessible and effective local services and attempts to find alternative ways of meeting the needs of individual service users.'

The state of social work, the growth of the third sector and 'volunteering'

Therefore, while community work survives through various forms of community development activity, CSW was swept away by the narrowing of social work's activity in the 1990s. This was marked by a return to individualist practice and, from 2008, an environment of austerity and a performance-led culture which meant that most activity was necessarily focused on crisis, with little ability to engage in preventative or even relationship-based practice (Ruch et al, 2018). The result has been demoralisation among front-line staff, rapid turnover and continued headlines undermining the profession's credibility (BASW, 2021b).

Back in the 1960s, the Seebohm and Kilbrandon reforms described earlier had led to the assumption by people within local authority social services that much of the work previously done by the voluntary sector would be taken over by the state (Brodie et al, 2008). Indeed, services for people with various disabilities was almost entirely taken over. This was to change in the wake of the NHS and Community Care Act 1990, when the private and voluntary sectors found themselves able to compete for contracts to provide services to local authorities in the new marketplace. The change from campaigning organisation to service provider was quite profound and made some of these organisations important players fronted by CEOs on very large salaries (Ferguson and Woodward, 2009; Turbett, 2023a). With governments keen to see the implementation of their policy commitments, the third sector allowed them to bypass local government and fund directly.

At the same time, policy pronouncements like Prime Minister David Cameron's 'Big Society' put an emphasis on communities providing services for themselves through volunteering (Turbett, 2014). The growth of volunteering and its place in providing preventative services has been enhanced by the employment by health agencies and the third sector (sometimes in partnership with social services) of 'community connectors' and 'community link workers', whose role is to refer people to walking groups and others concerned with healthy lifestyles. Other activities vary from community-run public toilets to libraries, usually replacing public services that have been cut by councils. Such activities frequently depend on third-age volunteers to provide the unpaid work that enables them to function, and one wonders how such services might function as demands increase along with the retirement age. CSW has a place for appropriate volunteering at the local level, but as detailed later in this book, the role of professionally skilled social workers who can use relationships well and recognise and deal effectively with the situations that inevitably arise should not be overlooked in the rush to provide services on the cheap through volunteering (Turbett, 2023a).

COVID-19 and the necessary rediscovery of community

The pandemic that swept across the world in 2020 saw the normal services that sustain communities shut down. In the UK, movement was restricted and access to essential amenities like shops and social gathering points was limited if not closed off completely. In this situation, and after many years of gradual decline of publicly provided community centres through austerity cuts, the idea of community hubs as local centres to access support, both practical and emotional, gathered momentum. Within a few months of the start of lockdown in the UK, about one million people had offered their services as volunteers (Marston et al, 2020). Coordination of their efforts was necessarily arranged on an ad hoc basis according to local conditions and the availability of buildings and staff who could be redeployed from other duties for the duration. Quite early on, a far-sighted blueprint that drew upon the experience of the HIV/AIDS epidemic of the 1980s was presented by authors from the Faculty of Public Health at the London School of Hygiene and Tropical Medicine and was realised in many localities:

- Invest in co-production.
- Fund dedicated staff and spaces to bring the public and policy makers together.
- Create spaces where people can take part on their own terms (for example, avoid bureaucratic formalities or technical jargon).
- Move beyond simply gathering views and instead build dialogue and reflection to genuinely co-design responses.
- Invest not only for this emergency but also for long-term preparedness.
- Work with community groups – build on their expertise and networks.
- Use their capacity to mobilise their wider communities.
- Commit to diversity.
- Capture a broad range of knowledge and experiences.
- Avoid one-size-fits-all approaches to involvement.
- Be responsive and transparent.
- Show people that their concerns and ideas are heard and acted upon.
- Collaborate to review outcomes on diverse groups and make improvements. (Marston et al, 2020: 1676)

This contains the kernel of CSW, and in some locations, social workers were central to such initiatives. In others, however, where continued statutory responsibilities were felt too important to involve more imaginative and creative deployment, this unfortunately did not happen. The pandemic did however bring the importance of community-based support back into the limelight (Turbett, 2021b).

The emergence of community as central to solving society's ills has featured in two popular and accessible books that have had an appeal wider than the usual academic and motivated practitioner audience. The first of these is Russell and McKnight's (2022) *The Connected Community*, which offers a basic guide to community empowerment for community activists and those who come in from the outside to support them – a concept they describe as asset-based community development (ABCD). The relevance of this approach to the social work task was highlighted in a guest blog by Russell on the official website of England's Chief Worker for Adults Lyn Romeo in 2016 (Russell, 2016). The other popular UK book is Cottam's (2018) *Radical Help*, which provides powerful evidence of the transforming power of community-based support for families whose lives are blighted by poverty and disadvantage. Cottam correctly describes social work in the UK as broken but goes on to describe how this might be fixed through community-based preventative practice. Both authors are recommended, particularly for those looking for basic explanations of the dynamics of community development and early family support, respectively. While Russell and Cottam have the ear of people in high places (Hilary Cottam was awarded an OBE in 2020 for services to the British welfare state), their impact as outsiders on the social work profession in the UK has been marginal. Both, though, have an important place within the broad argument for CSW.

Chapter summary

This chapter has provided an overview of CSW's origins in the post-war development of social work in the UK and how it rose briefly and unsuccessfully to prominence and then disappeared in the marketisation and focus on crisis-led services that predominated from the 1990s onwards. The chapter has argued that the move away from its key role in prevention and place within communities has harmed social work and reduced its support role for people in need. It has critically contended that the third sector has moved into much of the space formerly occupied by local-authority-provided social services and that, as a result of the attendant funding mechanisms, this sector no longer offers the campaigning challenge to the government and policy makers that it once did. Finally, the chapter has suggested that the recent COVID-19 pandemic demonstrated that locally organised services have strengths and potential that could be realised through CSW approaches.

Mention has been made of the idea of community orientation, the principal focus of the most recent literature (Pierson, 2008; Stepney and Popple, 2008; Teater and Baldwin, 2012) but an approach that differs in scale to that of the CSW model described in Chapter 3. Community orientation has a place in effective mainstream practice but, as we will see in Chapter 2, is required within the CSW model.

2

Bringing community into mainstream social work

Introduction: Why this chapter?

Perhaps it should not have been necessary to write this chapter: social work professional training may not focus much on community social work (CSW) (issues explored in Chapter 11), but its sociological content introduces the student to ideas of how opportunities are affected by class, place of birth, material well-being in childhood and other fundamentals. No one would question the importance of such teaching. However, as Fenton (2019) observes, many students still emerge from university with values reflecting their own background and not the passion for social justice that she rightly believes lies at the heart of social work. If this is true, then it is no surprise that newly qualified social workers may slide into the procedural assessment-based model of social work that is now commonplace, though thankfully not universal. This type of practice varies little wherever it is found, is often delivered from an inaccessible central location and is typically accessed through a call centre or in safeguarding settings through involuntary referral from other agencies (Turbett, 2021a).

The removal of the worker and team from the communities they serve has been intensified through the home and remote working that has become widespread since the pandemic. While home and remote working might have advantages for the worker, it undermines team identity, peer support, learning and relationship–based work, factors recognised in a review based on

29 inspection reports of English children's social services (Ofsted, 2022). In a time of cost-cutting to ensure that essential services are maintained by making savings, there are advantages to employers in reducing office capacity, with instant communication through digital technology available anyway. However, this reduction in estate, with its attendant hot-desking (loss of dedicated personal office space), is highly questionable in the case of social work. Workers who might live a long way from their workplace or community served are expected to make full use of digital technology to complete assessments and allocated tasks. How this can be achieved without the face-to-face contact that is at the root of relationship-based practice requires challenge.

Therefore, this chapter is necessary because of the barriers that are working against community orientation, be they ideological, educational or pragmatic ones based on cost savings or factors concerned with worker health and safety (during the pandemic) and misplaced worker convenience, or even dressed up with green credentials as reducing vehicle use. It discusses skills and practices for the individual practitioner that can be applied almost universally, without necessarily requiring the broader vision of a service or team that will be discussed in Chapter 3. In fact, it is argued that the practice approaches described form the kernel of the radical practice sought by those who are rightly critical of ineffective and even oppressive mainstream practice (Baines, 2007; Turbett, 2023b).

Community orientation explained

In Chapter 1, reference was made to Smale et al's (1988) list of what CSW is not, which is a good starting point for this brief discussion. CSW is a model that requires a team approach dedicated to the building of an alternative type of social work service built in partnership with the people in the community being served (this will be described in detail in subsequent chapters). Community orientation is simply practice that places emphasis on community and involves effort to build knowledge and networks that can assist personal support for service users. Hadley and McGrath (1984) describe the patch practitioners in Normanton as 'community-orientated' workers, but the term seems to have disappeared from the general literature of CSW after this. However, it is used regularly in the rural literature that emerged in North America and Australasia in the 1980s–2000 period (see, for example, Martinez-Brawley, 1982, 1990, 2000; Cheers, 1998, Ginsberg, 1998; Collier, 2006). The earliest of these texts links this approach to the Seebohm developments in the UK that placed community at the centre of social work delivery (Martinez-Brawley, 1982). Martinez-Brawley also discussed the notion of 'rural generalism' (the other rural social work writers echoed the theme); this suggests that good rural social workers are not precious about boundaries and will adopt any strategy that meets the needs of their rural service users in a context of sparsity over provision. This is often confused with generic working – the now almost defunct practice that saw neighbourhood social workers deal with issues from the cradle to the grave. Generalism, however, can be practised by workers coming from the usual service settings within children and family as well as adult services:

> The generalist considers problem solving on many levels, across a spectrum of conceptual and practical approaches, and pursues any avenue that may be productive. It is not a specific approach, like casework with its theoretical approaches. The generalist enters each situation ready to tackle an individual problem, a neighbourhood issue or a political contest. (Collier, 2006: 36–7)

Generalism has not quite disappeared from the UK's social work lexicon; a forthcoming book on rural social work practice describes its significance in detail (Pye and Turbett, 2024). The idea that if you are isolated from other professionals by distance and remoteness and there is a dearth of agencies to refer on to, then creativity and artistry in finding solutions is needed has as much resonance today as it did in the 1980s–2000 heyday of rural social work literature. The near disappearance of this genre, especially from the UK, has much to do with the trends described in Chapter 1 but now seems to be subject to a welcome rediscovery: the author is aware of networks in England and Scotland linking workers in rural settings where issues often neglected in mainstream social work narratives are shared, and the new book draws on such experiences.

It is worth interjecting here that there are settings regularly encountered that suggest themselves for community orientation regardless of the rural/urban context. The first of these concerns the placement of a social worker within a child's or young person's educational setting. Here, there will be an opportunity for creativity if encouraged and supported by those to whom the worker (and it is usually a singleton practitioner) is responsible. The other setting is that of the general practitioner (GP) practice or health centre, of which more is said in Chapter 6, offering an example from Northern Ireland.

Therefore, it is high time to rescue the terms 'community-orientated' and 'generalist' from the past and put them back into the centre of social work practice for the future, and they will be found throughout this book. They are not interchangeable terms: the former refers to the location of activity within the context of community; while the latter refers to the ability to work through traditional professional boundaries or specialisms to help create solutions to problematic issues.

The skills of the community-orientated social work case worker

If community orientation is to be effective, the worker who chooses to practise in this style should consider the skills they might need. Before looking at social work and community development skills, personal and professional presentation in a general sense is important in order to overcome some of the barriers that social workers commonly encounter due to their statutory roles. A good starting point might be to look at professionalism and how it might be interpreted – by both self and others. Despite the commitment of the profession to socially progressive values (expressed through professional codes and those of representative organisations like the British Association of Social Workers and the International Federation of Social Workers), there is still a belief by many social work writers that the 'culture of professionalism is conservative, self-interested and orientated towards the status-quo … professionalism is for social workers not for service users' (Mullaly, 2010: 120). In a slightly tongue-in-cheek parody of the Alcoholics Anonymous 12 Steps to Recovery, Mullaly (2010: 120) suggests that social workers embark on a de-professionalising programme that includes such admissions as:

- I came to believe that as a professional I could fix people and solve their problems.
- I came to believe that wearing expensive clothes and driving a fancy car did not separate me from my resource-poor service users.
- I admit to using professional jargon, acronyms, discourse and my prolific propensity for elite, exclusionary vocabulary to impress, overpower, intimidate and distance people.
- I admit to embracing professionalism without taking into account its undermining effects on my stated beliefs in social justice, egalitarianism, and other social work values and ideals.

The underlying message here is that oppression is often reproduced quite unintentionally and that approaches involving partnership with communities in finding solutions require conscious effort to address power differentials. We shall return to this theme later in the chapter when considering team culture.

Stepney and Popple (2008: 131) state that the practitioner's ability to critically think in the tradition of Freire and Gramsci is more important for the community-orientated practitioner than technical skills. Their contribution to community development theory and practice more generally will be discussed in Chapter 3, but their ideas fit here.

Paulo Freire (1921–97) was a Brazilian educator whose work among the poor and dispossessed of his country made him realise that it was their stories and experiences that held the key to change and improvement, not the imposition of ideology from outside. In two (of many) books, *Pedagogy of the Oppressed* (Freire, 1996 and *Pedagogy of Hope* (Freire, 1994), Freire discussed how education was not neutral and that just as it could be used to oppress people, it could also be an aid to liberation – a theory he termed 'critical pedagogy'. He applied this particularly to adults and used their stories and experiences to develop his ideas about pedagogy, in which his subjects were regarded not as empty vessels to be filled but as people with the potential to challenge the oppression that kept them poor and dispossessed. These ideas have been very influential on community work theorists like Margaret Ledwith (2020).

A major influence on Freire was the Italian Marxist philosopher Antonio Gramsci (1891–1937), who featured in the discussion about community and society in Chapter 1. Gramsci spent the most productive literary years of his short life in an Italian prison, and his prison notebooks, written between 1927 and 1935, were written in a coded form to escape censorship. Gramsci's main contribution to Freire's ideas was his belief that people were innately cultured and capable of critical thought but that this was blunted by those in power whose ideas dominated through the process of hegemony. Working-class people and peasants were stifled by their education, but when the situation was reversed and they were valued for their own contributions and their teachers assumed a facilitating role, they could develop their own consciousness and collectively challenge the hegemony of the ruling classes (Gramsci, 1982).

The ideas of Freire and Gramsci are important because they emphasise that change is possible and that this can be achieved through bringing people together in their communities and by facilitating their own expression and exploration of possibilities for making their lives better. While traditional casework theory puts the stress on the personal relationship between the worker and the service user, this borrowing of theory from radical and critical community development unleashes the potential for community approaches to meet the same objectives. Given that many people suffering poverty and disadvantage are from minority ethnic groups, mention must also be made of Frantz Fanon (1925–61), a psychiatrist from the French colony of Martinique who practised in Algeria at a time of its indigenous population's struggle for freedom from French rule. From his experience as an educated black man, Fanon explored how the native population's consciousness had been shaped by their white rulers, in his words, they wore white masks over a black skin but were made to feel constantly inferior to their white masters, to the extent that they embodied this into their psyches. In his role as a psychiatrist, freedom fighter and writer, Fanon sought to help victims become fighters against colonial rule and determine their own view of the world and their own futures (Fanon, 1965 [1961], 1986 [1952]). Fanon also commented on the brutalising process of racist presumption that colonisation has on the dominant white population. Fanon's writings are important in understanding how slavery and colonial rule have shaped racism and black experience and contribute to the necessary task of embodying postcolonialism into our anti-oppressive practice (Garrett, 2021).

The concept of intersectionality is important when considering oppression: this explains how power relations of race, class, gender and other differences overlap and intertwine to the benefit of the dominant group in Western society – the patriarchal power enjoyed by white men (Ledwith, 2020). Eddo-Lodge (2022) remarks that this issue of intersectionality is poorly understood by many white feminists when they fail to consider the situations of their black sisters.

Social work skills associated with community orientation need to be predicated by the 'joining skills' of 'empathy' and 'authenticity' listed by Smale et al (2000: 195). Both should address the insecure professionalism described earlier in the 12 Steps to Recovery programme. Empathy is the technical skill that workers need to consciously develop that enables them to listen, communicate feelings and express optimism that positive change is always possible. Authenticity is another value that needs to be learned individually: it cannot be prescribed by organisational ethos or stated sets of values; rather, it comes across through the ability of the worker to communicate interest and engagement through their behaviours and self-presentation. It involves honesty about power differentials and expectations, as well as congruence between what is said and what is done. Authenticity also involves awareness of non-verbal messages, including those given out by the worker: looking at one's watch (or mobile phone) might seem necessary for a busy worker but gives the service user a very negative message about their personal significance. Both are basic social work skills, though important ones in the inventory of the community-orientated social worker – skills that do not necessarily exist with volunteers and differently qualified individuals often nowadays tasked to work in communities with disadvantaged individuals and groups.

The following list offers a general skills inventory for the community-orientated social worker:

- An understanding of poverty, inequality and their impact on people's lives: such awareness needs to take account of how marginalisation in society arising from membership of a minority group – whether through ethnicity, sexual orientation or other perceived difference from white heterosexual UK culture and heritage – will exaggerate the impact of economic disadvantage (Mullaly, 2010; Wilkinson and Pickett, 2010).
- Lived or acquired knowledge of the community where activity is taking place.
- Network-building skills with both state and third sector agencies, as well as informal user groups.
- Basic social work assessment and relationship-building skills.
- An emphasis on the development of practice wisdom as a guide to situational response rather than a reliance on the techno-scientific knowledge that might be expected of, for instance, health professionals dealing with physical symptoms of ill health (Cheung, 2017). While guidance and procedural processes might be helpful, social work skill rests on acquired knowledge of relationships and how to use them positively. This involves creativity and artistry around relationship building and activities that can further casework aims (England, 1986): 'Creative expression is the hallmark of a good social worker' (James et al, 2020: 42). The use of theory is realised in practice (praxis) and otherwise serves only a very limited purpose in a helping relationship (but might be useful for formal reports).
- Humility and an ability to admit and correct mistakes.
- Ability to exploit and use the areas of discretion that exist in every setting that might lubricate processes and help enhance the experiences of both workers and service users (Lipsky, 1980; Evans and Harris, 2004; Turbett, 2014).
- Being a 'useful outsider' (Russell and McKnight, 2022: 139–41), serving while stepping backwards, working to reduce institutional dependency, cheering on community alternatives; being open and honest about what can and cannot be done,

affirming what communities can do for themselves, having a commitment to 'do no harm', being interested in community and not just reforming the employing organisation, and being courageous.

I have written elsewhere about achieving radical practice in mainstream workplaces (Turbett, 2013, 2023b). This involves consciously transforming workplace cultures in order to embed the possibility of doing things differently. There are several components to building team culture, some of which involve personal presentation (Baines, 2007) and others that concern collective approaches and opportunities for developing good practice:

- Seeking out workplaces with good supervision and workload management processes in operation. Without these bedrocks in place, the worker is at risk of overload and burnout. While supervision seems to be taken for granted as an important factor, workload management is often overlooked and, at best, substituted for by indicative caseload numbers (Miller and Barrie, 2022) that in themselves only tell part of the story about workload pressures (see UNISON Scotland, 2014).
- Seeking workplaces that offer the physical space for the creation and perpetuation of team culture. This involves workers having personal space (a desk) alongside other team members, though not necessarily in an open-plan setting – a factor that cannot occur through hot-desking (sharing a limited number of workstations and keeping personal possessions, paperwork and so on otherwise locked away). This facilitates mutual support and care for fellow workers, peer learning, and the sharing of stressful moments. Homeworking (a legacy of COVID-19) also works against the fostering of team culture.
- Challenging pervasive cultures that perpetuate oppression (Mullaly, 2010). This was touched upon when discussing Fenton's findings about graduating social work students at the start of this chapter. It requires the recruitment of allies and the skilled use of opportunities to question the assumptions that flow from mainstream politicians and media, for example: that the UK is being overrun with foreigners who are exploiting

our health and other systems (a myth with colonial and slavery origins underlying racism); that there is not enough to go round (the myth of scarcity); that information passed down through policy and other determinants is objective in form and should not be questioned (the myth of objective information); that all members of a certain group are the same (stereotyping); that people are responsible for their own oppression (victim blaming); and that human beings are competitive by nature and that class difference and hierarchy are natural phenomena (the myth of innate competition for resources).

- Settling down for the long haul: the building of a good workplace culture does not take place overnight and the worker engaged in this process needs to commit to this. Conversely, if barriers to change seem insurmountable, they need to leave and seek out a work setting with better possibilities.
- Avoidance of martyrdom: the worker who stands and falls on principles barely shared with others and draws management attention and disciplinary action might lose their job and will not be remembered for long. Battlegrounds need to be carefully chosen and the balance of forces measured before launching off onto particular campaigns that challenge the organisation. The worker-activist also needs to be in the majority trade union in the workplace and supportive of its significance and growth; this can offer not only protection but also a channel for campaigning.
- Building personal credibility and being likeable. Again, this will not happen overnight, but the worker who is known for their commitment and skill at the job will have a greater influence than the one who is simply good at offering challenge and critical argument.

While not claiming to embody all the qualities of the ideal generalist practitioner, I offer here two examples of community-orientated practice, both of which I was involved in personally. Similarly, I am sure that most of the social workers I have worked with in the past whose work I respect can recall examples of such practice; they are commonplace, if often unrecognised for what they are.

Community-Orientated Practice Example 1: Teenage alcohol misuse in a rural community

Social workers in the small rural team were picking up from vulnerable teenagers whom they were supporting that there was a growing issue with the dangerous misuse of alcohol. Networking with the local high school's staff and school nurse also indicated a more general concern about the trend. There were several cases of accident and emergency department (A&E) admissions involving young people who had consumed alcohol to a dangerous level. Parties were taking place that the young people described as 'empties'. Typically, parents were away overnight and believed that their young teenager was staying with a friend, while that friend, in turn, had told their parents that they were staying the night with someone else. This was replicated across the community, with few parents taking the trouble to check – a blind eye being turned in what was regarded as a generally safe community. Most parents were grateful at that time that their children were safe from what they perceived as the urban scourge of 'drugs' and saw alcohol as a safer option.

It was agreed in a meeting between the social work team manager, the school headteacher, the school nurse and the local police sergeant that an 'alcohol forum' would be established to meet monthly and work on the issue, involving the initiating group, a parent representative and an alcohol support service located some distance away that offered advice. The initiative was publicised in the local newspaper, and reasons were given for its formation. A presentation (by the school nurse) was made to parents attending parents' evenings in the school, and attention was paid to alcohol awareness in sessions she did with children at school. She obtained materials like 'drunken glasses' that the children could try on to give them the feeling of imbalance and nausea that comes with excessive alcohol intake. More as a gimmick than in the expectation that they would be used, parents in the school were given little credit-card-sized wipe-clean checklists for their children on which details of where they were and with whom could be entered, as well as whether parental consent had been checked (if they were going to another household). Within six months or so, some success was reported through feedback by social workers, teachers and health sources: 'empties' ceased, and there were no reports of A&E admissions. Clearly, the awareness-raising focus was effective and impacted in a way that an individual focus on the children whose behaviours were causing particular concern would not have done.

Community-Orientated Practice Example 2: A young women's empowerment group

A social worker in a seaside town suffering from post-industrial disadvantage, including widespread addiction to Class A drugs, was working in a children and family team concerned primarily with safeguarding issues. In discussion with her supervisor, she recognised that she knew several young mothers who expressed helplessness at their situations, particularly their abusive and drug-misusing partners. This was typically expressed in statements like, 'That's just the way it is round here' and 'The guys I know are all like that'. Of course, such statements have numerous dimensions, including the necessity of effective work with such men, but when this discussion was opened up at a team meeting with other social workers, several reported having similar disempowered young women within their caseload. It was agreed that a group would be set up and community learning and development colleagues (with whom there was little or no history of previous co-working or dialogue) would be contacted to provide a venue and support for the group. The social worker who had originally identified the issue was given some space (through workload management) to give to the task, as was a family care worker in the team. In conjunction with their community learning and development colleague, they planned a six-session group aimed at empowerment and consciousness raising. General subjects were introduced and discussed, such as 'Are men abusive?', 'What hopes do I have for my children' and 'What are the good things and bad things about our town?'. This enabled a safe space to share thoughts and experiences, and all but one of the women stayed for the entire six sessions. There was no formal evaluation, but the women involved all reported that they had benefitted and felt they had learned things that would help them make choices and achieve more control over their lives.

Is community-orientated practice effective?

Having effectively fallen below the radar from the 1990s onwards, there is no research base in the UK to help us determine the worth of community-orientated or generalist practice. However, a 2006 US study (Ohmer and Korr, 2006) looked at 269 articles published between 1985 and 2001 that focused on community practice using strengths- or asset-based approaches. Outcomes were evaluated based on their collective goals rather than those concerning individuals (improvement in community conditions over the well-being of individuals). The survey suggested that while success was reported in increasing citizen participation, which had a positive effect on those involved, less success was reported in influencing and improving the complex physical, social and economic problems of the poor communities typically subject to such interventions. Individuals benefited from improved self-esteem, personal and community empowerment, and leadership and political skills. Important considerations for collective social action building included the longevity of residence, commitment and sense of belonging (issues discussed briefly in Chapter 3). The article does not conclude that structural change was unrealisable but rather that it required further consideration. This is not dissimilar to the findings concerning the UK's community development projects (CDPs) of the 1970s described by Banks (2011; see also Chapter 1).

Chapter summary

This chapter has offered community orientation as a template for radical and anti-oppressive practice, that is, practice that takes account of context and works in a relationship-based and partnered way with people in the communities where they live and go about their lives. In doing so, it has proposed that such practice offers an effective bridge between critical and radical social work as a critique of social policy and actual practice in the real-life situations found in the mainstream of social work, including statutory settings. It has introduced the concepts of community orientation and generalism that underpin the individual practice that is essential in CSW and made brief mention of the important theoretical contributions of Freire and Gramsci in their development of critical pedagogy. It has suggested that community orientation and generalism are not dependent upon the presence of the CSW model, which will be outlined in Chapter 3, but as we will see, CSW is dependent upon practitioners with such qualities.

3

Community social work for the present era

Introduction

This chapter moves the narrative on to look at why and how community social work (CSW) fits with the requirements of UK society today and how social work managers and practitioners might consider moving the idea forward. This will be discussed in general terms; a more practical step-by-step guide will be provided in Chapter 12 of the book. While Chapter 2 focused on how community-orientated and generalist practice can be brought into mainstream casework-orientated settings by individual practitioners, this chapter will focus on what the author is keen to characterise as 'real' CSW: an approach taken collectively by an entire team focused on a particular community or communities (as defined in the introductory chapter). The changes required to adopt CSW cannot be taken without considerable planning, co-design and ultimately co-production involving community partners. Statutory social services and social work agencies still have responsibility for legally prescribed duties, including very important safeguarding ones, and care planning for vulnerable individuals, and these cannot be put on hold. Just because we believe that policy makers and agencies have become focused almost entirely on addressing the consequences of poverty and disadvantage rather than looking at its causes and how personal crises might be prevented does not mean that such activity is misplaced.

At the end of Chapter 1, it was stated that the three most cited recent books concerning community practice are concerned more with what is described as 'community orientation' than with CSW. However, despite the dearth of contemporary CSW literature, this chapter will draw upon two sources, neither of which mention CSW specifically, but both of which provide important material for our study. The first of these is the latest edition of Margaret Ledwith's (2020) *Community Development – A Critical and Radical Approach* because, although for a broad community-development audience, it highlights the most important considerations for effective, radical and challenging work in communities. Ledwith reminds us that this involves recognising the causes of the problems and issues commonly encountered in disadvantaged communities, the political context of such matters, and the need to incorporate such understanding in radical practice (practice that leads to change – personal, systemic and political). This is illustrated in the simple iceberg diagram in Figure 3.1.

The other text is Smale, Tuson and Statham's (2000) *Social Work and Social Problems*; the authors of which were all connected with the National Institute of Social Work (NISW) and its attempts to promote the Barclay Report's CSW in the 1980s (Barclay, 1982). However, 'Barclay' and 'community social work' cannot even be found in the index – as if the authors recognised the times they were in and that the CSW ship had sailed. Instead, they laid out all the components of CSW in a practical and concise manner (without the possible distraction of the label) to influence the new generation of care managers and risk assessors. While this might now seem like an accommodation, it is important to recognise that at that time, many nuanced writers saw potential in the individual focus of care management and integration with health services. These include Pierson (2008), who believed that integration with health offered a break with the siloed forms that social work service delivery had morphed into, which he blamed on the 1960s' legislation that had created vast and self-serving local government bureaucracies. It seems safe 15 years later to counter any misbelief that local partnerships would flourish, with the evidence of marginalised social services operating within very large top-down health-led bureaucracies described in Chapter 1. The premise of this book is that the direction of travel of the

Figure 3.1: The iceberg of disadvantage

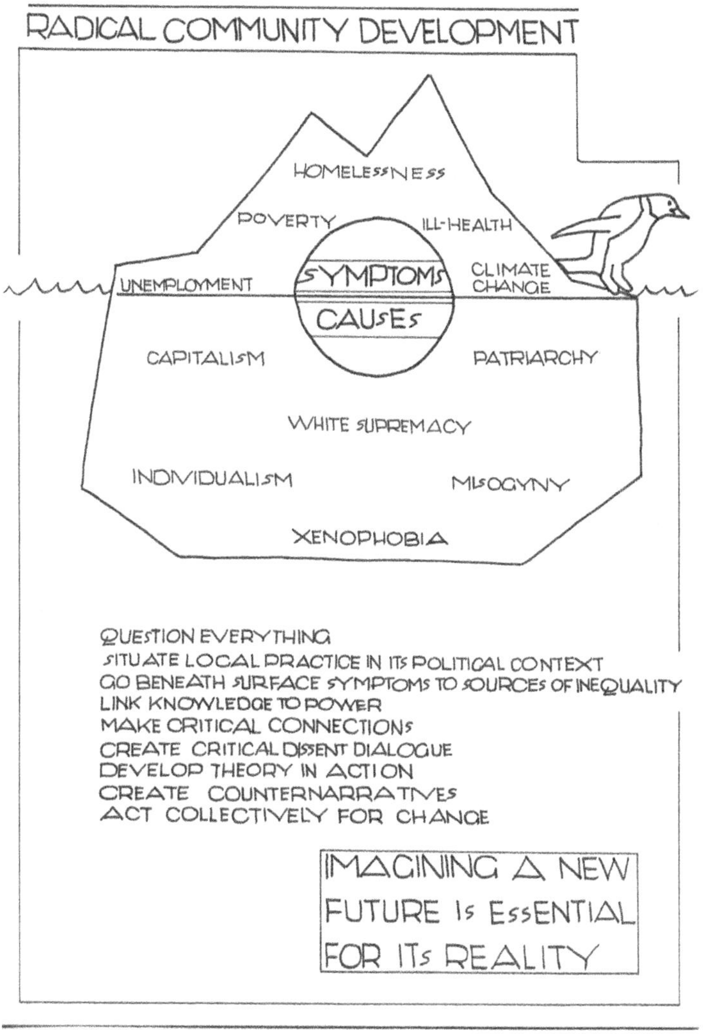

RADICAL COMMUNITY DEVELOPMENT

HOMELESSNESS

POVERTY   ILL-HEALTH

UNEMPLOYMENT   SYMPTOMS   CLIMATE CHANGE

CAUSES

CAPITALISM   PATRIARCHY

WHITE SUPREMACY

INDIVIDUALISM   MISOGYNY

XENOPHOBIA

QUESTION EVERYTHING
SITUATE LOCAL PRACTICE IN ITS POLITICAL CONTEXT
GO BENEATH SURFACE SYMPTOMS TO SOURCES OF INEQUALITY
LINK KNOWLEDGE TO POWER
MAKE CRITICAL CONNECTIONS
CREATE CRITICAL DISSENT DIALOGUE
DEVELOP THEORY IN ACTION
CREATE COUNTERNARRATIVES
ACT COLLECTIVELY FOR CHANGE

IMAGINING A NEW FUTURE IS ESSENTIAL FOR ITS REALITY

Source: Reproduced with permission of the copyright holder (Ledwith, 2020: 107).

profession in the UK has moved far from its values base in the 20 plus years since *Social Work and Social Problems* was written and that social work urgently needs a reset around CSW if it is to recover. The disguise is no longer necessary, and the valuable pointers in Smale et al's book can be stated for what they are: the building blocks of CSW.

Stepney and Ford (2000) propose an approach to working in communities based on six phases: familiarisation and information gathering; engagement and assessment; organisation, planning and partnerships; intervention in collaboration with community members; mobilising team resources for empowerment (of users and staff); and research and evaluation. The outline segments for the development of CSW that are explained in this chapter are not dissimilar but based on considerations that seem significant in the present era. These, in turn, cover themes around: the affordability of CSW; enabling and visionary leadership; community scoping for pilot/test of change; staff recruitment; networking and network building; initial steps and bottom-up participatory CSW creation; and, finally, evaluation.

Affordability: prevention is better (and in the long run cheaper) than cure!

Smale et al use a widely used analogy to mark out the importance of the preventative approach they describe (they do not say so, but it is commonly ascribed to Desmond Tutu, the South African cleric and anti-apartheid campaigner). They suggest that the specialist services that had by then developed in social work in the UK:

> were akin to a row of lifesavers lined up on a riverbank, each with a different colour of hat. None of them can enter the water unless the drowning person wears a matching colour. If their lifeguard is busy, people have to change the colour of their clothing to get saved. People without clothing that matches a coloured hat do not attract attention and are not rescued. Because, they, or their organisations, only get paid when they enter the water, none of the lifesavers go upstream. (Smale et al, 2000: 33)

Upstream preventative work is sensibly placed to intervene to stop people falling into the river in the first place and requiring later rescue: if we intervene before problems descend into crisis, we might stem social disintegration and save lives. The authors go on to develop the analogy by suggesting that the present emphasis of services means not only that people are not being stopped from falling into the river in the first place but also that it is not in the interests of the downstream lifesavers that they should, as this deprives them of purpose (and income!). Their efforts are anyway targeted at the individuals who fit their service eligibility criteria, and others are left to sink or swim until someone else (hopefully!) saves them. It seems doubtful all these years later that the analogy holds up completely: downstream services are under such pressure that upstream activity would surely be welcomed if it offered relief from the constant deluge of drowning people. It is useful, though, to highlight that there were managerial interests served by the direction that social work took in the 1990s.

While all this seems obvious, it might not be so to policy makers and budget holders, who are locked into a system where performance and outcomes are often judged by cost efficiency (with constant demands for savings through never-ending austerity) and immediate results. These concern the heavily criticised mechanistic performance-indicator systems that accompany managerial approaches, measuring outcomes through such matters as the volume of reports undertaken, cases opened and closed, waiting times, and other measurables (Harris, 2003). This reduced social work practice to a false set of technical competencies, whereas in reality, quality and effectiveness in social work intervention are difficult to measure; for children, this might have to wait until they are adults, and even then, there are so many variables, some of which (like brain damage or irreparable emotional harm) might have been determined prior to any social work intervention. A 2018 review in Scotland of attempts to address the issue suggests that while the profession seems to have moved beyond the crude managerial performance indicators of the 1990s–2000s era, the whole area is extremely complicated: any attempt to measure outcomes needs to take account of the client group involved and their fit with many other factors in the health, social and educational context of their lives (Smith, 2018). Later in this chapter, a suggestion will be made for how this might be achieved for CSW, but mention is made here because policy makers and budget holders will naturally want to know that any diversion of scarce resources will be worthwhile.

Our answer to this imponderable is to state our belief that it is not a question of 'Can we afford CSW?' but more one of 'Can we afford not to adopt this approach?'. The evidence for such a bold statement lies within well-researched evidence that the profession is failing in its mission within society (though much good work with individuals continues) and the workforce is consequently suffering (UNISON Scotland, 2019; BASW 2021a; Miller and Barrie, 2022). The idea of 'spend to save' is hard to sell in times of austerity but forms the basis of investment in upstream preventative services; the argument is that spending on creative services that prevent people falling into a downward spiral that leads, for example, to chronic ill health, addiction, family break-up, offending, institutional care and mental illness will pay dividends in the long term. All these crisis-led services are costly and often delivered through statutory duties to the extent that public spending must focus on them rather than on other matters, whether library services or fixing holes in the road. Despite this, it does seem that the idea of CSW is easy for politicians to grasp; in fact, easier to understand than very complex areas of mainstream social work – at least, that is the author's experience in Scotland of talking to politicians, from government ministers to councillors (more of this in Chapter 4, describing the Fife CSW team).

Leadership for CSW: top-down enabling for bottom-up building

While the whole premise of effective CSW is that it should be built through co-design and co-production in partnership with others at the base level, that will clearly not happen from within a public sector organisation of any type without the allocation of resources, involving senior managers with strategic and budget responsibility. It is they who will write the committee reports that will release funding. Qualified social workers are a scarce commodity, though experience suggests that recruitment will not be an issue when staff are offered the potential to be creative and are allowed to engage in the relationship-based practice they train for (on this, see the following chapters). Qualified social workers are an essential: they have the necessary professional training to assess issues, determine day-to-day interventions and evaluate and report on what is achieved (or not achieved).

As indicated elsewhere, recruitment and retention issues are inevitable unless the potential of staff is realised through changes to the working methods expected of them. In England, at least two authorities have removed the necessity to undertake procedural assessments and instead launched models that are based on ongoing conversations without predetermined outcomes. In Leeds, a lengthy assessment form for adults was replaced by a blank sheet of paper, on which the social worker was asked to write only what was necessary and outline solutions that were legal and affordable. The emphasis in the Leeds model of 'strengths-based social care' is on conversations rather than forms, looking at what people can do rather than at what they cannot (Leeds Council, nd). A similar approach has been adopted in Northumbria, which they call the 'liberated relational method', governed by 'two unbreakable rules – we do no harm and we do not break the law' (Changing Futures Northumbria, 2023). Such approaches are fundamental to CSW.

The CSW team might also involve others: social work assistants (or other para-professionals), group workers and community workers. Local circumstances will help determine the make-up of a team, but the experience of past initiatives and those described in Chapters 5–8 suggests that additionality is realised through the employment of people from within the communities that are the focus. Staff costs will be the major issue at the outset, as well as running costs. Imaginative and visionary leaders who see the potential of such approaches and who are willing to take on pragmatically minded colleagues competing for scarce resources are essential. Such leaders will need to be tactical and confident about CSW if they are to succeed. For this reason, CSW needs to be discussed as an idea worthy of attention at every level within the profession: conferences, professional associations and every opportunity available. While few at the top of the profession might openly challenge the idea of CSW, many will push it down the list of priorities when confronted with immediate demands for resources.

From a US standpoint, Hardcastle et al (2011) address this important issue for those who wish to turn social work practice back to communities. They discuss the notion of 'motivational leaders' (Hardcastle et al, 2011: 228) when considering the role of organisations: while charisma is fleeting and can result in deception, disappointment and loss of support, motivational leaders understand what motivates employees and how to lead to inspire motivation. Those in authority who govern without consent and support breed 'subtle non-compliance, sabotage, or open insubordination' (Hardcastle et al, 2011: 228). Public sector organisations are hierarchical and do not function along democratic lines; good leaders understand that dialogue and genuine consultation result in better compliance and motivation than dictates and sudden change. Hughes and Wearing (2007: 80) discuss the leadership traits of 'individualised consideration' (giving respect and responsibility to subordinates) and 'intellectual stimulation' (challenging subordinates with new ideas and approaches). An issue in social service organisations in the present era in the UK is that, as discussed in Chapter 1, senior managers may not have a social work background. This may or may not be a good thing: professional social work conservatism might hinder revolutionary change, but on the other hand, senior managers who have no experience of social work from the inside might also be defensive and resistant to innovation – though may not be, as they might see the potential of the CSW concept (I have certainly experienced this).

In addition, enabling senior managers need to trust staff with the concept of CSW and let them get on and build it themselves in partnership with the chosen community and its existing networks. Neither top-down control nor prescription will work for this model. Involvement in initial planning to ensure buy-in and understanding is required, as is continued interest in and support for staff, but over-control will inhibit the process of building, which will be described in the following Chapters 5–8. This can create what Banks et al (2003: 99) describe as 'ethical challenges': issues that might arise from conflicts of interest when community participants are invited to take some control over their lives. This involves careful negotiation but, above all, confidence

Figure 3.2: The cycle of top-down/bottom-up leadership, co-production and co-design

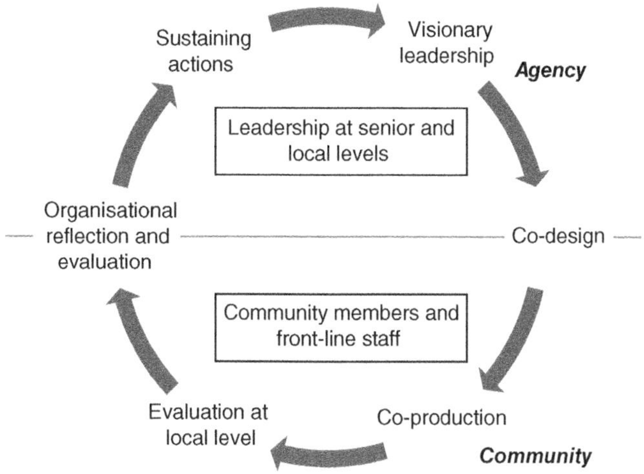

Source: Colin Turbett

in the professional values and integrity of the staff involved. Figure 3.2 demonstrates the continuous cycle of top–down and bottom–up leadership and how it promotes the co–design and co–production of services for CSW.

Identification of the target community and community profiling

This section starts on the basis that CSW is likely to emerge in a locality as a pilot (or test of change) rather than as part of a comprehensive reorganisation (in fact, this is preferred, as it will enable learning to accumulate and errors to be addressed and rectified). The organisation that chooses to go down this path will need to choose the community or geographical area (which might contain several communities) carefully. To win political support and funding, it is likely that an area that scores highly on indicators of poverty and deprivation will be chosen; this may or may not already have known features that support community identity or cohesion. Factors to consider from the outset are:

- Is this a defined geographical community?
- Is this a self-identified community whose presence crosses boundaries of place, for example, an ethnic group?

Once the community has been identified, initial background work will include:

- The history of the community: for example, if post-industrial, what were the obvious features that bound people together in the past and might be disappearing or absent in the present day, for example, workplaces, trade unions, social activities and so on?
- Who might be considered to bring into the initial planning stage of the initiative to offer local knowledge and insight: the list might include local councillor(s), school headteacher(s), identifiable community leader(s) and so on; prescription is not offered here, as this will depend on personality, obvious interest and support for the idea. A planning group might emerge from this trawl.
- Background statistical research: sources would include demographic information from the Census and the official indices of poverty, which are collected regularly and published. This will provide information on population make-up and highlight imbalances or obvious factors for attention, such as a preponderance of under-16s or over-65s. Such information can be useful to realise funding opportunities.

The next stage of preparation will involve a more serious community profiling that digs deeper into issues identified at the initial stage. Ledwith (2020) suggests that this might be a participatory process of co-production. This is implicitly supported by Smale et al (2000), whose basic premise is that once we begin to identify social problems, we must base our formulation on 'joint enterprise': the formulations of users as well as professionals. While this should be borne in mind, it perhaps belongs at a later stage; again, we would not want to be prescriptive. If, for instance, the community concerned is an ethnic group, it would be a mistake not to involve key members or representatives from the earliest stage. If it is a geographical community, it is suggested at this early stage that the planning group gathers basic information and data surrounding concrete community assets: schools, community meeting places, shops, libraries, the third sector presence and so on. Community profiling can be a small-scale exercise (typically given to social work students as a task). It might be a major community planning piece of work involving systematic data collection through quantitative research alongside the gathering of views and ideas through questionnaires and other qualitative methods (Hawtin and Percy-Smith, 2007). This is not suggested here – though CSW might be the result of such an exercise. Community profiling as preparation for CSW is a simpler exercise concerning the gathering of enough information to better understand the nature and identity of the locality chosen.

Hardcastle et al (2011: 96–7) also suggests that for a geographical community, attention is paid to resident type. Perhaps using language more familiar in the US, he suggests that there are five: 'drifters' (less than five years' stay and likely to move on), 'settlers' (less than five years' stay but likely to stay), 'relocators' (more than five years' stay but likely to move on), 'natives' (more than five years in the community and unlikely to move away) and 'dreamers' (those who live in the community without investment and would like to be somewhere else). Consideration of these typologies might involve some local variation, but it might be particularly helpful when considering rural communities, where the poor are often displaced by financially secure incomers who can dominate local discourse (Pye and Turbett, 2024).

Team recruitment and induction

Managers responsible for the CSW initiative will need to select staff to take the project forward. Again, we cannot be prescriptive but suggest, as outlined earlier, that core staff are qualified social workers led by a social-work-qualified team manager. They and others should be recruited based on their own interest rather than involuntary redeployment. They should ideally bring different life and work experiences and might include those with lived experience of the community being served. While commitment is always sought by those recruiting staff, people are obviously free to move on as they wish, and this will always be an issue, especially for a pilot/test-of-change initiative with only a short guaranteed life projection. Probably the most important quality sought at the recruitment phase is interest in being creative and innovative and not relying on day-to-day activity being based on endless assessment production.

Induction training for the selected team will involve an introduction to the history and ethos of CSW. Table 3.1 on transition is based on one that appeared in Hadley et al (1987) and has been reproduced since in the existing UK literature. It illustrates how change can be made from traditional casework to CSW. While the model suggested in this book involves a pilot/ test of change rather than the transition that the model suggests, it is useful to help staff appreciate the changes in approach required.

Staff also need to develop community development skills (the subject of an accredited post-graduate course for social workers in Northern Ireland [see Chapter 11]) and groupwork skills. These can be developed over time but need to be recognised as important changes from the traditional assessment and casework skills that qualified social workers will have learned through professional training. Groupwork texts are in abundance, but recommended for CSW because of its participatory and self-directed premise is that by Mullender and Ward (1991: esp ch 2) for its detailed advice for workers approaching this for the first time. These authors identify five 'practice principles':

1. Refuse to accept negative labels: all people have skills, understanding and ability.
2. Service users must always be given the right to decide whether to participate in self-directed work, and the right to define issues and take action.
3. Practice should reflect understanding that problems cannot be seen purely because of personal inadequacy – oppression, social policy, the environment and the economy are major contributory forces.
4. People acting together can be powerful: groups can help people gain that power.
5. Practice what you preach: non-elitist principles mean that workers do not 'lead' the group and use their specialist skills and knowledge to enable people to make decisions for themselves

Table 3.1: The transition from traditional case management casework to CSW

Characteristics of traditional casework	Characteristics of CSW practice	Changes required of practitioners
Reactive: help is requested or given through statutory referral when the individual's situation is in crisis and normal helping networks are unavailable or failing	Preventative/proactive: the practitioner intervenes before a service is demanded, before the situation has deteriorated to a point of crisis or serious safeguarding issues, and while potential still exists for the use of the user's network for agreed support	1. Reduction of reactive responses and their replacement with proactive ones 2. Reduction of case-by-case approaches based on the work of the individual professional and the growth of teamwork and collective responses 3. Close interaction with the community
Arm's length and not easily accessible: practice is dictated by bureaucratic processes and assessment tools prescribed by the agency through legal and policy obligations and often delivered centrally from locations not easily accessed by service users	Services close to the community: services are accessible and practice is defined by the living conditions and environment of users and their social surroundings	1. Creativity and artistry in local programmes formulated to meet agreed needs 2. Individuals are considered holistically and not according to service-user label or group 3. Recognition of the importance of informal networks 4. Sharing of professional responsibilities
Professional responsibility: the social worker carries a caseload for which they are individually responsible and accountable	Shared responsibility: the practitioner shares responsibility for finding solutions with the user, their networks and natural helpers, as well as their community	1. Practitioners replace their individual responsibilities (caseloads) with activities and supports in partnership with users and other agencies 2. Development of groupwork and community development skills
Individually focused: the principal target of intervention is the individual service user, with assessment focused on their individual problems, the degree of pathology and the risk to self and others	Centred on the social network: the target of intervention is the social network – both the personal and wider community one – of the service user, with assessment focusing on the distribution of responsibility and capacities for change, both individually and in the wider networks and agencies operating in the community	1. Development of skills that strengthen and support carers and social networks that mitigate individual need

Source: Colin Turbett adapted from Hadley et al (1987).

and acquire such skills themselves. All work must challenge oppression: whether through race, gender, sexual orientation, age, class, disability, or any other form of social differentiation upon which spurious notions of superiority and inferiority are built and kept in place. (Mullender and Ward, 1991: 30–1)

A good example of CSW groupwork is described by Berry (cited in Wroe et al, 2019), involving a group for asylum-seeking women in Manchester known as 'Rise and Shine'. The women, some recently released from UK immigration detention, were from Bangladesh and a number of African countries. The story of their meetings, which took place infrequently, demonstrates facets of Freire-inspired activity and ideas that suited the different cultural backgrounds of the participants: structured sessions in a warm and welcoming venue with children being cared for elsewhere; the sharing of food prepared for the occasion; and the swapping of stories and experiences. Interestingly, effort was made for the women not to regard themselves as necessarily the vulnerable victims of trauma but, through the building of a trusting environment, to challenge themselves and move beyond their comfort zones.

For community development, the already cited books by Ledwith (2020) and Craig et al (2011) are good – the latter for its overview of issues and history. Radical community development, Ledwith tells us, has four key components:

• It is a political activity: 'If people are prevented from reading, meeting together, questioning and organising, they fail to make connections between the overlapping, intersecting forces of power that result in multiple oppressions of class, race and gender acted out through capitalism, imperialism and patriarchy' (Ledwith, 2020: 82).
• It is an educational activity: knowledge is the basis of action, and community development is partly about inviting people to learn by asking questions and seeking answers (as per Freire's social pedagogy described in Chapter 2).
• It is a theoretical activity: again, after Freire, it involves the unity of theory and practice in action (praxis). Ledwith decries the absence of a popular counter-narrative to that of the neoliberal

view of the world projected, for example, in the tabloid press and through social media. This, she argues, highlights the need for theory as a foundation of positive social change.

- It is about collective action for change: people acting in concert with one another can make connections across boundaries and traditional social barriers and together exercise power to challenge the status quo and achieve change.

While Ledwith describes a template for a radical approach to community development, the voices of those encountering and suffering from the worst disadvantage (those who might seek social work support) can be empowered through CSW to make a valuable contribution to the process of change. The phrase 'community capacity building' should be mentioned in passing here: it began to appear in the late 1990s through Labour policies at the time of the Blair-led government and is often used in policy documents and change strategies. While Craig (cited in Craig et al, 2011) considers that it is no more than a policy rebranding of community development, he associates it with top–down models that might be thought of as the manipulation of communities to fit government policies and programmes; in that sense, it has brought back to life tensions previously experienced in the field of community work.

In Chapter 2, an explanation was given about the importance of fostering a good team culture. This applies absolutely to the building of an effective CSW team. where creativity and artistry are celebrated, along with a collective endeavour built around a strong value base. The team members need to work alongside one another (remote and homeworking do not fit with the nature and relation-based activity of CSW) so that shared reflection and peer support are part of everyday experience. Team meetings should be regular, and individual reflective supervision should be accorded importance.

First steps: the blank sheet of paper and redesign of social work

As will be seen in Chapter 5, the Fife Council initiative involved giving the team that commenced the project a 'blank sheet of paper' to go out into the community and see what they found. This involved quite intense networking from the outset. This foundation-laying aspect will vary from community to community but involves knocking on doors and opening up conversations with potential partners: social housing providers, the police, school headteachers, third sector agencies located in the community, health agencies (general practitioner [GP] practices and community nursing teams), churches, local authority agencies (especially community learning and development or equivalent) and, last but not least, statutory social work agencies. If not already involved through the initial discussion process described earlier, local councillors and other political representatives should be consulted. Management committees of social and community facilities in existence in the area must be involved through early dialogue. This will involve selling them the idea of CSW and winning their support on the basis of the possibility of their participation. This will all involve confidence about the task and a degree of bravery in approaching people in various settings, some of whom will not have had a good experience with social workers in the past.

Some clarity about networking is needed: here, we describe and celebrate horizontal ties that are created locally, not the vertical protocol-ridden systems that are negotiated at a level remote from communities and then handed down for front-line operationalisation. Horizontal networks are less likely to reflect power differences and can in fact countervail these when they exist (Hardcastle et al, 2011). Examples of such inhibiting top-down systems abound in the structures created in the UK to integrate health and social services organisations that fail to deliver the expected efficiencies and improvements for patients and service users (National Audit Office, 2017; Miller et al, 2021; Turbett, 2021a).

Out of local conversations, a plan should begin to emerge about where and how to start engaging with community residents through the effective use of relationships, winning trust and showing interest in all areas of life, not just presenting problems. Relationship-based practice has already been highlighted in this book as a significant component of CSW (and indeed good social work generally):

[Relationships] are not in and of themselves therapeutic or, necessarily, beneficial to the participants. It is the nature and quality that matters. ... Good relationships take commitment, hard work and imagination; when they work, they can offer a vulnerable or emotionally damaged person the possibility of encountering themselves in a new and positive way, a chance to see themselves through different eyes – perhaps for the first time, as someone worthy of another's interest and respect. (Ruchman et al, 2018: 281)

From a grounding in the research information already acquired, the issues in the area will become clearer, as well as the role the CSW team could play in helping address them. From this networking comes the network building that begins engagement with the community. The tasks of social work must be put forward as a prime purpose of the CSW team; this is not principally about broad community development, though aspects of that might well follow. Smale et al (2000: 34–6) remind us that a turn to community involves a balance between 'aid and development'. Social work's primary tasks include:

- protecting vulnerable people at risk of abuse (safeguarding);
- maintaining people in their own homes wherever possible, and arranging alternatives if required;
- helping improve and sustain positive individual and family functioning;
- creating systems that enable people to control their own lives, for example, self-directed support; and
- working to reduce the incidence and impact of anti-social behaviour.

CSW might include all these 'aid' matters but will go further than them to look at collective solutions and the development of communities to enable mutual aid and support between community members. This will include environmental improvements that benefit all (for example, by reducing anti-social behaviour). An overarching objective is that of community well-being rather than just benefit to the individual who happens to be in receipt of social work support; this is what Smale et al mean by 'development'. To residents of a deprived community more familiar with social work being about intrusion and social control, the idea that social workers want to help and support people can come as a welcome surprise! Other agencies too will be pleased at the absence of bureaucratic referral systems and the informality that should surround CSW. A community police officer working alongside the Fife CSW team described the ease with which he could share issues with staff as "social work off the books".

This setting aside of the traditional case management/caseload model lies at the heart of CSW, with its de-individualisation of commonly encountered problems. This does not negate the need for individual support when required, as people experience issues in different ways: some will be more adversely affected than others and will require support. A CSW approach might identify supportive responses from within the community but will not avoid a personal service by a social worker if this is agreed as necessary.

Presentation and language

CSW is fundamentally about changing the direction of social work to one of support, partnership and prevention, and with this comes a new approach to the people we work with. Among the new ways of seeing relationships described throughout these chapters comes a consideration of the language we use. Just as CSW is a move away from the consumer–purchaser–provider neoliberal framework that has done so much damage to the profession, it has to involve new ways of describing the partnership with people. This is not just about avoiding and calling out oppressive language (described in Chapter 2) but also about addressing the hidden oppression of 'us and them', that is, the 'expert professional' and the 'uneducated' service user. Language can humanise but also dehumanise (James et al, 2020). Vita Snowden, the convenor of the British Association of Social Workers (BASW) CSW Special Interest Group, talks of replacing the word 'service', which has neoliberal contractual connotations, with 'activity', which implies a journey we make together. Activities, she goes on to say, fall into 'sessions' rather than 'programmes', again moving away from the notion of a contractually provided service. The people whose needs require our services, through no fault of theirs but often because of the circumstances they were born into, deserve dignity and respect. As also said in Chapter 2, power differentials, particularly for social work staff with statutory duties involving safeguarding, cannot be wished away but should be explored honestly and openly – put on the table at an early stage. Partnership too has its boundaries in real terms: the late neighbourhood worker and ex-social work academic Bob Holman lived and worked in the same locality in Glasgow, drawing a minimal salary and sharing much of the daily experience of those he was helping (*The Guardian*, 2016). We cannot expect community social workers to replicate his dedication, but as stated in Chapter 1, there are means of self-presentation that de-professionalise in the sense of breaking down obvious barriers.

Darren McGarvey (2018: 79–80), the Glasgow writer who experienced poverty and disadvantage on a personally damaging scale, warns about the dangers of organisations 'parachuting in' and minimising partnership in pursuit of externally presumed goals:

> For locals who wish to engage, it leads to a sense that privileged people with little insight into their concerns are being parachuted in to superimpose their values onto everyone. Projects that are rolled out in this way are less about identifying the community's shared aspiration than about deciding what the community needs and then corralling, manipulating or compelling people towards it.

McGarvey (2018: 79–80) was discussing 'arts, the media, charities, and NGOs … behaving … much like an imperial power', but his message is clear and applicable to clumsy attempts to apply CSW using pots of government money designed to meet policy objectives. This book will demonstrate that partnerships start with listening to what people have to say about their communities rather than imposing the concerns of well-meaning and temporarily funded visitors.

Pursuing policy initiatives

CSW teams are in a good position to engage with community members in pursuance of the establishment of initiatives generally considered to be worthwhile and progressive. Indeed, they can act as a bridge between the often remote organisations trying to implement policy and the vulnerable people they are hoping might benefit. There are examples easily found in current practice:

- Personalisation/self-directed support: notwithstanding budget issues, there are often difficulties in identifying choices for individual disabled and vulnerable children and adults who are eligible for personal budgets so they can maximise levels of independence (Gardner, 2014). CSW team staff intimate with local communities and their resources are in a good position to both identify and even create resources where these are needed.
- Family group conferencing (or family-guided decision making): this originated in New Zealand and was based on Māori culture, where families are central to problem solving. It is now in widespread use in the UK for addressing issues concerning children, involving trained staff who help extended families evolve plans to address issues of concern to professionals (Edwards and Parkinson, 2018). CSW teams who know their communities and networks are in a good position to facilitate this process.
- Parental advocacy: this has the same roots as family group conferencing but concerns parents of children subject to safeguarding and child protection processes, possibly involving the child's removal. Offering parents advocacy from trained and paid independent advocates (with an emphasis on those with lived experience) has had some astonishing results in keeping children with their families and promoting positive change. Over many years in New York, it is credited with reducing the looked-after population from 50,000 to some 8,000 children (Tobis et al, 2020). The model is now spreading throughout the UK but requires local effort to embed, and CSW teams are again in a strong position to promote and create local networks.

Reflection and action

Schön's (1991) reflection-in-action/reflection-on-action framework is well known in social work education and describes the process through which practitioners both learn as they go along through what is essentially trial and error, a practice that becomes automatic as experience is gathered, and then go on to consider matters systematically after an event or process. Given that contemporary CSW does not have a wealth of proven and research-based literature and experience upon which to draw, this is essential for a new initiative. Time needs to be set aside for a team to think collectively about how plans and interventions have or have not been realised, how and why changes have taken place, and whether these met the original objectives. Once confidence has been gained, this can involve partners and community members. A record of deliberations can assist evaluation. If resources allow, this process could be extended properly into a piece of action research involving other participants in the community (Westoby et al [2019] describe an action research example from Australia that used critical pedagogical approaches). Action research could describe the team's journey and trace matters of potential interest, such as the use of discretion (referred to in Chapter 2), unforeseen barriers, enabling factors and other issues affecting success or otherwise.

Evaluation and telling the world!

The question of the measurement of outcomes was discussed critically earlier in this chapter. Clearly, while measurement and evaluation are much debated and crude performance indicators have largely been discarded, the evaluation of the quality of work of a CSW team presents as even more problematic. Numbers of 'cases' dealt with in the traditional user categories (children and family, vulnerable adults, and so on) do not apply in the same way, and neither would any numerical measurement. There are more participatory ways of evaluating quality: feedback questionnaires are universally and extensively used in the retail and service sectors, as well as public service organisations, so much so that many people become tired of being asked to complete them and, if they do, answer in a perfunctory manner. However, the feedback gatherers will use what they get to either reflect positively on their customers' experience or introduce changes to accommodate popular preferences. This does not fit with the ethos of CSW, where community members are not customers (as they were described in the business styles that crept into social work in the 1990s), and unless service users are particularly motivated, this method might be of limited value.

Properly resourced qualitative research will tell funders and policy makers much more and is likely to capture elements of the relationship-based nature of CSW. Given that CSW is still rare in inception, it might be possible to draw an external funder interested in social work development to pay for university-based research. There is a crossover between evaluation, feedback and finding means to tell others about the merits of CSW; these might range from co-produced videos to written material aimed at different audiences, including community members, politicians, local activists and the social work profession more generally, as well as academia. The opportunity to speak to others at conferences and professional gatherings also has an important place. The author has been involved in various such presentational and promotional efforts (see the References and Chapter 4).

Statutory responsibilities

The teams that pioneered conscious and deliberate CSW in UK local authorities in the 1980s' era took on statutory work – a more natural development in the days of generic social work before this was completely overtaken by specialisms (as commented upon in Chapter 1). The landscape has changed: now, social work teams operate alongside each other delivering different statutory tasks along different organisational lines, sometimes working for different bodies and often not sharing geographical boundaries. If CSW is to be true to its premise as a relationship-based preventative and community-led service that seeks to walk alongside people and communities, then it cannot and should not see itself as yet another specialism. Not only is this leaving colleagues already suffering from unrewarding crisis-driven work to more of the same, but it lends itself to the potential for conflictual division within organisations, communities and indeed the profession itself. In whatever way it starts, and it is recognised that this may be staged (as in the Fife model described in Chapter 5), the assumption of statutory duties should be a goal if not determined as an immediate responsibility. The danger in not doing so is that CSW is seen as a diversion of resources in hard times rather than a solution to social work's present crisis (as seen in Northern Ireland [see Chapter 6]).

Chapter summary

In contrast to Chapter 2, which focused on how a motivated individual practitioner might carve out space for creative community-orientated practice, this chapter has focused on building CSW as a planned and concerted team approach. It has assumed that this will be done on a pilot/test-of-change basis by the public sector organisation that organises social services in the area concerned. While emphasising that this involves non-prescriptive but locally conditioned top-down enabling and bottom-up building, it has offered a systematic approach to planning and executing the model that should fit most situations, whether involving a geographical neighbourhood or a dispersed community of interest, such as an ethnically minoritised group. Chapters 5–8 will describe efforts to create CSW and community-orientated practice across the four jurisdictions of the UK, and Chapter 4 will set the context for this discussion in legal and policy terms.

4

Policy drivers and relevant legislation in the UK

Introduction

This is a problematic chapter to lay out: by the time it appears in print, policy changes through the electoral process may well have altered what was current at the time of writing. It is nonetheless important to map out what drivers exist that might further community social work (CSW) and what might be used to promote it, or at the very least suggest it as a strategy that fits. As social services policy making is devolved to the governments in Wales, Northern Ireland and Scotland, each jurisdiction (administration) will be examined separately. The Westminster Parliament presides over social services issues in England, as well as some welfare and overarching economic and fiscal duties in relation to the whole UK. The chapter will try to unravel some of the apparent complexities in a manner that will be relevant for at least the immediate future. The aim here is to offer some pointers about policy and legislation that might be used to argue for resources to create CSW approaches within social services organisations. Detailed discussion of all the legislation governing social work and community development is beyond the scope of this book.

Overarching past UK legislation of relevance are the Human Rights Act 1998, the Equality Act 2010 and the Child Poverty Act 2010. The latter set targets for the eradication of child poverty that were to be pursued by the devolved parliaments (for a brief guide to social work legislation across the UK, see Turbett, 2018a).

This general discussion must start with an overview concerning context: although some are devolved, general tax-raising powers remain in the hands of the UK government in Westminster, which then allocates funding for the devolved governments to determine how to spend on the responsibilities they hold. The overall pot is determined by the Westminster allocation, which since 2010, has been affected by continued rounds of austerity. Although the value of these grant allocations has consequently reduced, wealth for a minority has increased dramatically, with an attendant increase in inequality and demands on welfare services (Dorling, 2018). Local governments, which remain responsible for the operational delivery of social services in England, Wales and Scotland (the situation differs in Northern Ireland, as will be explained), are in turn restricted by the amounts they receive from the government, which have also reduced over the years quite markedly as a consequence of austerity. Therefore, such discussion always comes back, most would argue, to resources and the lack of them; supporters of the neoliberal Westminster Conservative governments in power for over a decade since 2010 would suggest that choices made by the devolved administrations and then in turn by local governments are of at least equal importance. However, the right-wing idealogues who have been influential in Westminster since 2010 are in favour of low taxation, an unregulated free market and the lowest possible levels of public spending (Dorling, 2018). Such thinking presents obvious barriers to innovation in providing social work services at a local level if additional resources are required.

England and the Westminster government

In 2010, shortly after election as prime minister, David Cameron made a speech where he outlined his vision of the 'Big Society'; this heralded an initiative whereby communities would be given more powers, people would be encouraged to volunteer, responsibility would be transferred from central to local governments and support would be given to co-ops, mutuals, charities and social enterprises. Although this seems in keeping with some of the premises of CSW and community development outlined in this book, the policy was a response by the government to austerity and shrinking public expenditure. The message was that it was everyone's responsibility to create thriving communities and not the state's, which should reduce so that citizens might be 'empowered'. The following year, spontaneous riots broke out in various cities following the police shooting of a black man (Mark Duggan) in London. The report published in the wake of the riots into their cause and meaning highlighted the fact that the poor and dispossessed felt no part of British society and needed more than just encouragement to volunteer to do so (Turbett, 2014). The policy was quietly dropped in 2013.

Within a few years, politics in England became overwhelmed with arguments surrounding 'Brexit', that is, whether the UK should remain part of the European Union. In many forgotten former industrial areas typically far from London (the centre of the wealthy finance sector), where poverty and hopelessness were endemic, promises were made by 'Brexiteers' that 'taking back control' of the UK would mean an end to unwanted immigration (blamed for a dearth of employment and opportunity) and prosperity based on the release of public funds for regeneration and improvements in the health service. This all resulted in a wave of support from areas in the North of England that had solidly voted Labour in the past for Johnson's Conservatives and a landslide victory at the 2019 general election. The policy consequence of this new-found commitment to help areas of the country that had escaped the prosperity enjoyed in traditional Conservative-voting regions was 'levelling up', which was announced in the Tory manifesto of 2019. At the time of writing in 2023, this policy is the subject of a parliamentary bill: the Levelling-Up and Regeneration Bill under the auspices of the levelling-up minister who presides over the Department of Levelling Up, Housing and Communities (formerly known as the Ministry of Housing, Communities and Local Government) (UK Parliament, 2023). The aim to reduce 'imbalances' seems clear in the title and has won cross-party support, though Labour has described the Bill as weak in delivery. The Bill's proposals are not about reducing inequality (which might involve such things as increasing the tax burden on the rich) but instead about a hope that the funding of projects in poorer areas of the country will create prosperity. Much of the Bill's proposals concerning local democracy are about bureaucratic changes designed to strengthen the hand of councils by sharing responsibilities and authority. Other detailed aspects concern the democratisation of planning regulations. There is nothing proposed that empowers local communities to determine and co-design the services they receive. Levelling-up funding seems restricted to physical infrastructure projects rather than community assets, so in all, there is little in this that might facilitate a turn towards community in social services delivery.

Over the years of Tory government, there have been initiatives aimed at supporting vulnerable families, most notably the Troubled Families programme that started in 2011 as a response to the urban riots of that year. This initiative claims (and this is disputed) to have helped over 400,000 families between 2015 and 2021 through some £1.5 billion of spending that has changed the way they are supported in areas that have taken advantage of the funding through a variety of locally shaped initiatives (UK Government, 2021). The programme has been criticised for locating problems within families rather than within the context of wider social and economic issues (Bonell et al, 2016; Crossley and Lambert, 2017). However, the opportunity for funding preventative programmes that adopt a CSW approach seems possible.

The Care Act 2014 was introduced on the basis that it replaced various pieces of legislation that covered services for adults and their carers. Although there was little that was new, Part 1 of Section 2 of the Act empowered local authorities to organise services on a preventative basis, but the detail did not state that this might involve new initiatives and emphasised the avoidance of duplication and use of the voluntary sector (UK Government, 2014). However, the Care Act (UK Government, 2014: Part 1.1, Part 1.2[i]) starts with the positive statement that 'the general duty of a local authority ... in the case of an individual, is to promote that person's wellbeing'; the detail focuses on individual care needs but includes 'the individual's contribution to society' – the premise of a community-orientated service.

Children and family social work in England is governed by the Children Act 1989 and various associated pieces of legislation that have updated it (UK Government, 2023). Section 17 of the

Act empowers local authorities with a general duty to provide support to children in need and their families, but in practice, this is subject to eligibility criteria and the availability of resources. Children's social care services were the subject of an independent review published in 2022 (UK Government, 2022). While the report acknowledged the need for preventative relationship-based practice that harnesses community support, it suggested achieving this through targeted family support and made no reference to the need to tackle collective issues surrounding poverty and deprivation. In this respect, it ignored the scoping review of children's services in England by the British Association of Social Workers (BASW, 2021b), which recommended exactly that through CSW. The independent review's findings and recommendations were very much in line with the Tory's Troubled Families approach referred to earlier.

The principal opposition to the Tories in Westminster is the Labour Party. Their range of social policies was announced in May 2023 and might be expected to form the basis of government strategy should they win power in the upcoming general election. Plans are outlined in the documents 'Safe and secure communities' (Labour Party, 2023a) and 'Public services that work from the start' (Labour Party, 2023b). The former is very much about tackling anti-social behaviour and crime in communities and, as well as populist commitments to increase police numbers and stamp down hard on offenders, includes a welcome commitment to restore youth services and listen to community voices about community-led strategies. 'Public services that work from the start' talks about increasing prevention in healthcare but does not discuss social services provision in this regard, though it does commit to listening to communities (Labour Party, 2023b). Here, it seems, if Labour's commitment to dialogue is genuine, are potential opportunities to talk about CSW in England with policy makers and politicians.

Wales

Uniquely in the UK, the Welsh parliament (Senedd Cymru), established in 1999 (with devolved powers to create primary legislation since 2011), has brought together the various components of social services legislation into a single act: the Social Services and Well-Being (Wales) Act 2014. The Act includes among its principles two that are of relevance:

- Prevention and early intervention – increasing preventative services in the community to minimise the escalation of critical need.
- Co-production – encouraging individuals to become more involved in the design and delivery of services. (SCW, 2022)

A recent evaluation of the Act's impact suggests that Wales is beset by the same adverse issues and consequences facing social work delivery as described for the UK generally in Chapter 1. Among the findings are the following statements summarising users' experiences:

- tokenistic approaches to listening.
- power imbalances between themselves and professionals.
- the need to chase social services for support and recognition.
- cultural insensitivity. (Welsh Government, 2022)

There was also a finding that user involvement in the co-production of services was poorly understood despite documentation in policy and legislative guidance. Examples of the Welsh government's commitment to the principle of co-production include the requirement for regional partnership boards to ensure that users of care and support 'must' be actively involved in 'assessing need, strategic planning, service design and delivery' (Welsh Government, 2020). In February 2023, regional partnership boards adopted a charter for 'service user, third sector and provider members' in order to ensure all members could 'effectively inform, influence and be involved in the design and delivery of services' (Welsh Government, 2023).

The principles of collaboration and involvement are espoused in the Wellbeing of Future Generations Act 2015 as a tenet of sustainable development. An emphasis on user involvement is also reflected elsewhere in legislation, such as the 2015 Prudent Healthcare policy in relation to health services and the introduction of the Citizen Voice Body for health and social care in the Health and Social Care (Quality and Engagement) (Wales) Act 2020 (Welsh Government, 2022). As elsewhere, the ability to match aspirations with action has been affected by a lack of resources, but the policies underlying legislation certainly suggest potential for the development of CSW initiatives, and this is evidenced by the developments in Torfaen and Carmarthenshire described in Chapter 7.

Scotland

Against a background of continuing debate around extending devolution to full independence, the Scottish Parliament have been very busy passing legislation since its establishment in 1999. Depending on definitions of social work interest, over 20 pieces of social work legislation have been passed, and the process continues with proposals to launch a national care service. Scotland, unlike the other devolved administrations, continues to include criminal justice within its social work remit. At the time of writing, the Social Work (Scotland) Act 1968 continues to be the bedrock of legislation. However, the Section 12 promotion of the social welfare aspect (referred to in Chapter 1) and the similar Section 22 duty in the Children (Scotland) Act 1995 are regarded as discretionary powers rather than absolute duties and have suffered over the years due to resource deficits. As elsewhere in the UK, these statutory powers and duties have been overtaken by funding opportunities made available directly from the central government, for example, 'Troubled Families' funding in England and the 'Enabling Neighbourhoods' and 'Families and Communities' funds in Scotland. Another fund of relevance is that associated with The Promise Scotland, which is available for innovations that (in broad terms) act preventatively in communities to keep families together (see Chapter 5). While aiming to encourage innovation and efficient services targeted where they are most needed, the effect of this kind of funding method has been to diminish the role and direct funding of local governments and increase the power and authority of national and very large third sector organisations (for a critique of this in Scotland, though valid for the rest of the UK, see Turbett,

2023a). Of course, the opportunities provided should be used where appropriate.

The main general policy driver for community-based initiatives in Scotland comes through the Community Empowerment (Scotland) Act 2015. This is a wide-ranging piece of legislation, the main aim of which is to encourage the community ownership of land and assets and to ensure a community voice in the shaping of public services. The Act places duties on public authorities that contribute to community planning to engage in community planning partnerships, which are supposed to determine outcomes for local improvement. The reduction of inequality is given prominence. The main inspiration for the Act was the findings of the Christie Commission of 2011, a Scottish government-sponsored report that was, and remains, influential (Scottish Government, 2011). In addition to a desire to empower local communities, Christie's key priorities, almost a manifesto for CSW, included:

- Recognising that effective services must be designed with and for people and communities – not delivered 'top down' for administrative convenience.
- Working closely with individuals and communities to understand their needs, maximise talents and resources, support self-reliance, and build resilience.
- Prioritising preventative measures to reduce demand and lessen inequalities. (Scottish Government, 2011: ix)

The Scottish government is controversially planning to usher in a national care service with, at the time of writing, a published draft bill, which is largely enabling in content (Scottish Government, 2023). The proposals, which followed a government-sponsored report (the Feeley Report) published in 2021, came out of the 2020 pandemic and were a response to the high mortality rates of residents in care homes (Scottish Government, 2021). While the report focused on care homes and adult social care, the proposals as discussed so far suggest far-reaching organisational reform of all social work and social care services in Scotland. There is nothing in the Bill that promotes CSW, but the opportunity to argue for this within the context of previous policy commitments is obvious.

Northern Ireland

Northern Ireland is defined by a very long history of division between its two principal communities, one of whom held political dominance until fairly recent times. That division descended into violence ('The Troubles') as the dominant power defended its authority and the oppressed group sought justice. While a popularly supported peace has reigned in relative terms for the past 30 years, the divide sadly continues. One of the consequences of division between people in localities that considered themselves under siege was not only a strong sense of community and identity but also, in the poorest places where services were most needed, a commonly held feeling against state interference in personal and local affairs. All that history may be a reason why CSW enjoys greater influence there today than anywhere else in the UK.

While Northern Ireland enjoys devolved government in theory, in practice, failures to agree over constitutional fundamentals have resulted in suspensions of the Stormont Assembly and prolonged periods of direct rule from Westminster. This has stifled the legislative reform and modernisation seen in other parts of the UK. It has also arguably left civil servants and local officials to create policies without much in the way of political interference.

The main legislation governing Northern Ireland is itself a child of The Troubles: Direct Rule, alongside the need for reform, resulted in the unique system of quasi-autonomous agencies that brought together health and personal social services in a unified structure (created through the Health and Personal Social Services [Northern Ireland Order] 1972). Initially, four health and social services boards were established in 1973, but the system has since evolved within integrated structures in line with trends that came from the UK government and were evident in the organisation of healthcare elsewhere: there are now five health and social care trusts in which all public sector health and social care staff are employed. While this has given impetus to the goal desired elsewhere of health and social care integration, it is not considered to have benefited children and family services (Jones, 2023). These are provided through the trusts under the terms of the Children (Northern Ireland) Order 1995.

A number of official policy documents in Northern Ireland have called for community development approaches to be embodied in social work and social care. Notable are the 'Power to people' report of an expert advisory panel on adult care and support (Kelly and Kennedy, 2017) and, from a health and well-being perspective, the 'Expansion of community development approaches' report of 2018 (Northern Ireland Department of Health, 2018).

In 2018, the Department of Health for Northern Ireland authorised pilots for general practitioner (GP) practice-based primary care multi-disciplinary teams (MDTs) throughout Northern Ireland (Northern Ireland Department of Health, 2019). The purpose and rationale are described as follows:

> A new model for primary care multi-disciplinary teams has been developed which is seeing local GP practices focus not just on managing ill health but also on the physical, mental and social wellbeing of communities.
>
> Research suggests that up to a fifth of GP time is spent on social issues that are not principally about health, with GPs not always best placed to address these issues which may be underlying ill health. Practice-based social workers have therefore been recruited. (Northern Ireland Department of Health, 2019: 12)

These commenced in 2019, and at the time of writing, some are in their fourth year. The MDTs bring together various disciplines, including physiotherapists, social workers, mental health practitioners, health visitors and district nurses, with an emphasis on prevention and early intervention and the time to spend with patients (that is, relationships). Each MDT has at least one qualified social worker, banded at the senior practitioner level, amounting to about 80 in total. However, another important recent official report, the *Independent Review of Children's Social Care Services*, questions the use of the scarce resource of social workers in MDTs when children's front-line services are struggling with staff shortages (Jones, 2023: 146). The same report, however, and very positively, recommends and makes a strong case for children and family social work in Northern Ireland to transform and become community based. This clearly presents an opportunity to reimagine social work along the lines of a CSW approach, and activists in Northern Ireland might want to start thinking about how they can be proactive in this process. Jones makes the point, shared by many in social work and social care in Northern Ireland, that services are generally undervalued and under-resourced, pointing to how, as elsewhere in the UK, integration with health has resulted in absorption by the larger body rather than true partnership.

Introduction to Chapters 5–9

Having described the policy context that might encourage a return to preventive and relationship-based community practice in the UK, Chapters 5–9 will offer some examples from across the four countries. These do not follow a set format, as each describes very different settings and contexts and so follows its own individual course in terms of description. This also reflects the way in which their stories were told to the author and the information was made available, with systematically consistent research and evaluation being beyond the scope of this book. They do, however, offer a flavour not just of what is happening but also of what is possible. They will be followed in Chapter 9 by a reflective overview of what they tell us and what lessons might be of use elsewhere.

5

Scotland: Fife Council's community social work team

Introduction

This chapter will describe the story behind the formation of the Fife Council's community social work (CSW) team in 2021 and its history up until the time the book was completed. The chapter includes a substantial contribution from Molly Crombie, a social worker within the team. The author has been involved with the Fife CSW team on a mostly informal and voluntary basis since soon after it became operational in 2021, acting as a critical friend and keen advocate of its sustained development. The chapter features several titled policy initiatives and funding streams, some of which are local to Fife; the reader is asked to bear with this, partly because they are important to Fife workers and managers but also because they illustrate the complex mechanisms sometimes needed to get CSW off the ground.

The vision and the realisation

The Fife CSW team's story starts with the move to the council of Kathy Henwood as Head of Service for Education and Children's Services, Justice and Social Work (and Chief Social Work Officer), in 2019. Kathy, who brought experience from both statutory social work and voluntary sector settings, was keen on returning social work to communities. She believed that this could relieve pressure on statutory teams, bringing closer connectivity between families and social workers, but was under no illusions of how difficult it might be to convince immediate colleagues of the wisdom of such a strategy. One of her first organisational changes was to capitalise on the work done to bring about a 'Return to Fife' (expediting young people's plans to return to their families and local communities from expensive placements outside of the council's area) and investing in 'Belonging to Fife', building resources around family and community-facing supports to enable children and young people to remain in their families and communities. This was difficult but was achieved, releasing funding that she was keen to invest in a CSW initiative. At the same time, various Fife Council services in the Kirkcaldy area were working together on a 'test of change' initiative to align responses to high levels of vulnerability and need in the area: 'Putting People First'.

Kirkcaldy, with a population of about 48,000, has traits of post-industrialisation, being a former centre of coal mining and linoleum manufacturing: the former has ceased, and the latter is a shadow of what it was, with decline bringing a reduction in population from the 1970s onwards. Within Kirkcaldy are pockets of very high levels of need, particularly in the Gallatown and Sinclairtown Council housing schemes, with scores that rank them among the 5 per cent most deprived areas in Scotland according to the Scottish Index of Multiple Deprivation. The CSW initiative brought with it local funding opportunities and fitted with other policy drivers: the council's own overarching strategy, 'Plan for Fife; the Scottish government's 'Tackling Child Poverty Delivery Plan'; and 'The Promise', a widely publicised national strategy for improving the lives and outcomes of looked-after children in Scotland. This was also a time when services were emerging from COVID-19 – again, an opportunity to try to do something new to meet the needs of communities that had suffered over the previous period and were now facing a cost-of-living crisis. The plan from the outset was to create a new team through (initially at least) the short-term secondment of staff, including qualified social workers, and let them loose to build a service alongside local partners. The first appointment in May 2021 was of a service manager to provide direct management and support the creation of the CSW team: Karen Pedder was a former service manager of operations at Fife Education and Children's Services, with considerable experience of the hard end of social work and a commitment to try something new.

Therefore, at the time of the project's creation, the stars aligned in Fife: a budgetary opportunity alongside national and local policy drivers, but most of all, a visionary leader prepared to meet the challenge of sceptical colleagues with a service that lacked any very tangible evidence base. At this time, there were no other such CSW initiatives in Scotland involving local-authority-employed qualified social work staff, though there were a number of initiatives aimed at bringing services closer to communities but focused on statutory service delivery (including in Dundee Council, Moray Council and Angus Council).

The blank sheet of paper

Karen Pedder soon set about gathering what information about CSW she could find and appointing staff; there was no shortage of applicants, and the initial team began operating in August 2021, consisting of two social workers, a social work assistant and two team managers (to meet commitments made to partners through the 'Putting People First' joint test-of-change initiative). New job descriptions for the posts were agreed with the council's human resources staff, differing in emphasis from those in statutory teams and their focus on 'assessments'. The new team immediately set about spending time to get to know the selected areas in East Kirkcaldy, including the village of Dysart – a former mining community where people were said to feel quite forgotten. This involved building relationships with the agencies already there, determining how to reach out and commencing conversations with community members. The headteachers of two primary schools were keen to be involved and offered space to develop parent hubs that would be open at set times each week for parents to meet with the members of the CSW team. The focus of these was to promote discussion about the respective neighbourhoods and what they require. CSW staff were also there to help with individual problems and issues. The hubs took off well and became popular and welcome venues for individuals, some of whom had previously struggled with social isolation and personal difficulties. Several expressed initial surprise, based on their own experiences with children and family services, that social workers could be helpful, supportive and non-threatening. Relationships with other agencies grew to the extent that confidence was built in making informal approaches about situations of concern that the team might help with. This was favourably described by a community police officer as "social work off the books". The team's approach was very much one of quiet but continuous development, with regular self-reflection and consideration about where to take things.

The winning of political support would be crucial to the team's survival and progress into local communities. In February 2022, a webinar took place to which elected members of Fife Council were invited, along with chief officers and anyone else from the council who wanted to find out more. This was well attended and included input on the general reasoning for, and history of, CSW (by the author), as well as a presentation by the team about their activity and successes up until that early point. Several of the councillors representing different political parties expressed enthusiasm for the initiative. It seemed clear that they grasped its meaning quickly and could see potential benefits – in some cases, at least reflecting the issues brought to them by constituents that were not easily resolved by referral to existing services.

Out of the early presentation of issues by community members and existing agencies, workstreams quickly emerged. These could not have easily been predicted: a lack of diversionary activity for those on the edges of addiction issues and petty crime led to the formation of a bike group, while service to a hidden cohort of teenage school refusers led to a public library-based group and a positive impact on school attendance. Socially isolated individuals whose issues fell between the cracks of mainstream services were identified (sometimes discovered through the school hubs, food banks and other gatherings that team members attended), and individual support was offered with some good outcomes. The team grappled with issues surrounding recording: very much wanting to move away from traditional bureaucratised methods, they maintained a diary of activity, alongside minimal records of personal support offered. If issues were identified requiring referral to statutory teams, 'warm handovers' were planned and carried through.

The National Conference, November 2022

Soon after the successful Fife webinar aimed at an internal audience, plans commenced for a Scottish national conference to both showcase the team and promote the CSW model. I was very much involved with the six-month planning process, alongside Kathy Henwood and Karen Pedder. Kathy was able to interest some influential keynote speakers, including Chief Social Work Adviser to the Scottish Government Iona Colvin, as well as Fiona Duncan, the well-known public face of The Promise initiative. Karen set about planning input from the team and the community members and partners with whom they had been involved. My own role was to promote within the wider social work community and identify other speakers and workshop presenters whose input would be of maximum relevance.

The conference was a great success, filled with practitioners from across Scotland, as well as practitioners and partners from Fife. The event drew heavily on the experience of Scotland's neighbours in Northern Ireland, both in terms of a keynote by 'Community Development in Social Work Practice' course leader Fergal O'Brien (see Chapter 11) and workshops by a third sector organisation working with older people in North Belfast and multi-disciplinary team members from a large general practitioner (GP) practice in Derry (the Clarendon Practice, featured in Chapter 6). The most inspiring session of the day was a panel discussion featuring Fife CSW team members, community partners and parents from the Dysart Primary School parent hub, who gave strong accounts of their learning and positive experience over the previous year. The same parents also helped produce a video that was shown at the event, which also contained some powerful stories (see later). The conference certainly helped put CSW on the map in Scotland and consolidate its place in Fife. Several Fife councillors who attended were inspired enough to commit to seeking funds for the CSW team to extend to their own areas outside Kirkcaldy. In addition, at least one Scottish local authority began to look at how they might establish a CSW team. Fife staff have also been involved in presenting workshops on their experiences at national conferences in Scotland, England and Northern Ireland and have spoken to undergraduate students in two universities in Scotland.

Growth and the future of CSW in Fife

Between October 2022 and March 2023, additional funding enabled the recruitment of more social workers and social work assistants. By this time, there had been staffing changes, as two of the original team members had moved on for various reasons. However, recruitment was never an issue, and a mix of experienced staff and newly qualified staff from different backgrounds joined the team – some in time to attend the National Conference. Their interview process involved some of the service users with whom the team had engaged. New workstreams emerged, some through ideas raised by staff and agreed after team discussion. After staff changes, most for personal reasons but some because of continued uncertainties surrounding the team's long-term future, the team's establishment (at the time of writing in August 2023) consisted of a team manager, senior practitioner, seven social workers and six social work assistants. All bring very different skills, life experiences and interests, which are encouraged through the system of using 'proposal forms' for new ideas, which are then considered collectively.

The increase in staffing allowed the planned growth to proceed, including a move into a new geographical area, Cowdenbeath, at the request of local councillors. How the move to Cowdenbeath started, and how it was seen by the team itself, is richly described by one of the social workers, Molly Crombie:

> 'After a successful pilot in Kirkcaldy, the community social work movement in Fife has gained momentum and support on both a local and wider scale. The approach has gained support from practitioners, community members and from local politicians. So much so that the Cowdenbeath Area Partnership Committee voted to include financing the community social work service from its "community recovery" funding.

Prior to any engagement in the area, data and statistics around possible opportunities for intervention were collected in order to justify the introduction of community social work. The figures highlighted great areas of need for intervention. These included low school attendance, high unemployment, mental health issues and substance use. However, aware that numbers and statistics only tell you so much, we endeavoured to learn more about the history of the area, gain an understanding of the community itself and what people who live and work there think and experience.

To achieve this, our first step to developing the CSW approach in the Cowdenbeath and Benarty area was to undertake an extensive scoping and mapping exercise; we used this as a means of putting boots on the ground. Our approach was to explore the area, popping in on local groups and services to show face and introduce ourselves. We also made appointments with relevant professionals that hold a key role in the area, including schools, community learning and development (CLD), housing and third sector agencies. Through this, we met with key professionals, elected members, organisations, community groups, families, children and young people in the area. The aim was to understand the current service provision landscape: what is available to people and where are the gaps? In other words, who does what, where do they do it, what service do they provide and are people in the community accessing it? This involved such activities as having a cup of tea with the caretaker in the local community hall and handing out food-bank packages while chatting to families about what brought them there. It also involved meeting with the local councillors to discuss common themes they are presented with by constituents who are requiring support.

In alignment with Fife Council's "no wrong door" approach, it is an intrinsic part of community social work to be in the spaces that people of the community frequent, use and feel comfortable in. The service delivery landscape in a community can often be complicated to navigate, for families and professionals alike, with services becoming ever more unobtainable. This due to their retreat into inaccessible, corporate buildings and the list of criteria and threshold becoming a far reach from an individual or family requiring some basic support. The current financial landscape demands an individual or family to be in crisis before allowing access to a social work service, and by then, they have no choice but to cooperate. It is essential in community social work that the support should be where people need it, when they need it and through their own choice.

The main objective of the community social work team intervention in the Cowdenbeath area was quite simply that skilled and qualified social workers are present within the community, delivering early and preventative social work services that are visible and accessible. It was arranged, at management level, for the team to join local partnership groups and meetings to ensure coordination of new initiatives in the area, driven by current policy involving consultation and co-production. This also ensured there was no duplication of services. It was during the development of these professional relationships that it was agreed we could be co-located with other professionals, such as CLD, housing, communities, to make multi-agency collaboration easier.

During our research, it became apparent just how intrinsic the mining history of the town was to the identity of the individuals who live there. The area remains resilient, strong and united in their approach to community and looking after each other. So much so, it didn't seem as if there was much room for external service delivery to take place in the area. Many of the services we visited were run, staffed and funded by local people for the benefit of others in the community. This suggested that any approach to fundamentally improve the life opportunities of individuals in this area must be done with the people who live there: "with, not to", which is exactly in alignment with community social work values.

The writer Darren McGarvey [2018: 98] comments that organisations who enter impoverished communities "rarely encourage self-sufficiency. Rather the opposite, each engagement and intervention creating more dependency on outside resources and expertise, perpetuating the role of the sector, rather than gradually reducing it."

Although we are creating roots to become a permanent part of the social work sector in Fife, we are under no illusion that the funding is precarious. Furthermore, the delivery of services is forever at the mercy of the ever-changing financial and political priorities of central government. The combination of this, alongside the complex relationship this mining town generationally has with the local authority and their desire to keep service provision internal to the community, increased the need for a co-produced approach. As such, to ensure we are contributing to lasting change for these communities, we are prioritising an approach typically more associated with CLD, which means collectively focusing on community empowerment. This includes a focus on education, agency, control, voice, community strength and the creation of constituted groups. As a team, we undertook voice community engagement training to be able to support communities to achieve ownership, aiming to create constituted groups that work for the best interests of the community.

This approach, however, takes time. It takes the building of trusting relationships, and it takes confidence, power and learning. So, this will not come fast and easy. In the meantime, we are operating a split delivery model: running hubs, where we are present in places that people frequently use, such as community centres, food banks and schools. These hubs are used by people on a drop-in basis to discuss pertinent issues to them at that moment in time. We also offer enhanced support that is a more direct and intense approach, working with an individual or family over a longer period to address identified goals. This work typically takes place within the person's home as well as in the community. Individuals and professionals in the area have been informed of where and when the hubs take place, so they can turn up or signpost someone our way for support. Furthermore, there is an option for individuals or professionals to refer themselves or someone they feel requires support. This can be done through the duty phone line or email and only if the individual has provided permission for us to engage with them. They also must be able to identify certain goals that they wish to work toward with the support of CSW. On occasions that we are unable to provide support to an individual, we can offer advice and signpost to other services that may be able to help. Advice is available to all individuals and professionals, making CSW a visible, accessible community resource.' (Molly Crombie, July 2023, personal correspondence with the author about the team's experience of the move to community social work.)

Evaluation

The team have faced difficult questions from colleagues elsewhere about how they evaluate and measure outcomes for individuals as well as the community. Traditional evaluation methods involve addressing such outputs as the number of assessments produced, case conferences held, children on child protection registers, individuals provided with care plans and so on. Clearly, these do not fit a CSW team who, at the stage described, are not carrying statutory cases (though an increasing number of individuals with complex needs are being given 'enhanced support'). The team have tried to address this by devising a set of outcomes based on the Scottish government's well-being indicators (themselves based on the concept of 'gross national happiness' as a challenge to 'gross national product' as a measure of a nation's well-being). These, as can be seen, are applied to the community rather than the individuals with whom the team are working, whose progress is seen through a collective structural rather than simply individualistic prism. This is a work in progress but illustrates the move from an individual casework to a CSW approach:

- living standards
- health and psychological well-being
- how people spend their days – involvement in community
- education
- community vitality
- good governance
- environment and culture

The team also gather performance information relating to numbers: groups and other community places attended; individuals provided with advice and support; and meetings for networking purposes. Individual stories are also recorded, so that communities can see themselves reflected in the service, and feedback has been sought voluntarily for external scrutiny purposes. The two stories here were provided by service manager Karen Pedder and illustrate the team's approach and how this is evaluated.

Story 1: Andrew

'Andrew was an adult male who was introduced to the community social work team by the 'safer communities' officer in the area. Andrew had relocated to Fife from England and was living in temporary housing accommodation. He had an enduring mental health condition, and his resulting behaviours were becoming problematic in the neighbourhood, resulting in the threat of becoming subject to an anti-social behaviour order.

There were various professionals involved with Andrew but we found he was living in sparse and poor home conditions with no utilities, no cooking facilities and minimal household essentials. The property required a number of repairs to maintain his safety and wellbeing, but it appeared these issues were not being adequately addressed.

Andrew was not registered with a GP so was unable to obtain essential medication to manage his mental health condition or access medical care which only compounded his difficulties in the community.

Numerous referrals were made by the Safer Communities Officer to the social work contact centre requesting support from adult social work services, however these requests were declined as preliminary assessment indicated Andrew did not meet the three point criteria for adult protection and support.

Community social work team actions
- Timely response to initial request for involvement.
- Supported multi-agency partners who were involved to agree and co-ordinate next steps and actions.
- Assessed risk to Andrew and staff involved with him.
- Liaised with area adults social work team to further explore eligibility.
- Built relationships with Andrew through persistence and creative means despite failed visits and lack of initial engagement.
- Used social work knowledge of services to identify correct health expertise and access to assessment through in-patient care and a co-ordinated treatment plan.
- Practical help with food, fuel, and essential household items.
- Liaison with the responsible services to maintain property and ensure utilities were in place.
- Provided a bridge to longer term tenancy support and supported relationship building between Andrew and involved professional team around him.

Outcomes evidenced
- Community social work assisted other professionals to have an increased understanding of the bigger picture for Andrew's situation using a holistic

approach as opposed to testing his needs against a threshold criteria.

- Identified individual goals, strengths, talents, and interests.
- Urgent house repairs reported and completed – creating a home.
- Medication plan in place and Andrew's mental health stabilised with a co-ordinated plan in place.
- Benefits entitlement checked and PIP application completed.
- Strategies to support completion of daily tasks implemented.
- Sustainable sources of support to access food and fuel were identified for times of crisis.
- Tenancy support established.
- Professional agencies seen to be working together better.
- Andrew had increased capacity and was linked into the local community to be able to pursue his talents and interests.'

Story 2: Sheila and David

'Sheila was a single parent with the sole care of her 11yr old son, David who was on the autistic spectrum. The family had been known intermittently to the children and families social work service for a number of years.

David had a number of social difficulties and during the pandemic, school became a major issue. Sheila felt she could not return David to school post-pandemic and was trying her best to meet his educational needs at home. This was however becoming an issue and a concern as he would soon be transitioning to high school.

Sheila had had some difficulties with her relationship with social workers in the past and there was a concern David might become involved in the child wellbeing process or even be subject to a referral to the Children's Reporter.

A "warm handover" was arranged by the educational psychologist between Sheila and the community social work team to ascertain whether an early intervention approach could prevent the family moving into statutory measures.

Community social work team actions
- Time spent building relationships with Sheila and David.
- Identified methods to communicate and engage with David using his interests in football and wildlife.
- Agreed goals with Sheila and David together.
- Breaking the cycle of social isolation for both Sheila and David by creating informal support networks in the local community.
- Liaising with the educational psychologist to agree a transition plan for re-integration into education.
- Supporting Sheila to identify and pursue her interests and 'hear her story' and life expectations.
- Identified and developed Sheila and David's strengths.
- Liaised with children and family's disability team to undertake s23 assessment.

Outcomes evidenced
- David linked in with Raith Rovers football club and plays there several times a week.
- David attends YMCA [Young Men's Christian Association] bike club.
- Improved social development for David who now has a wider support network.
- David now in school full time for the first time ever and able to manage and negotiate conflict if it arises.
- Family diverted away from involvement with statutory services.
- Sheila states she feels listened to by social work and has control in her life.
- Sheila pursuing her own interests and has increased self-efficacy.

- Sheila feeling less stressed and anxious about the parenting role.
- s23 assessment being completed which will provide the opportunity for specialised support.'

As mentioned earlier in this chapter, the team have also produced two videos that include testimonies from community members they have worked with. The accounts of people involved in the school parent hubs typically start with an expression of surprise that social workers are actually there to help people – a perception based on previous dealings with, or perceptions of, mainstream children and family services. One young single parent, Mary, whose personal and family life was on a downward spiral, describes her own journey over the previous year, which illustrates several unique ways in which the team work: being there when people need them; being approachable; working with the individual's perception of the help they need; and sustaining that support. As Mary states:

> 'I've been attending the hub for about a year now. To start with, when I was asked about the hub [by the school headteacher], I said I wasn't too sure. I came along and was quiet to start with, and Leanne [team member] approached me, and then Lisa [another team member] approached me, and then I had a chat with Lisa on stuff that was going on. They've supported me quite a lot throughout this year. They've attended appointments with me; they've been there to speak to when I've struggled. Personally, just for me, if I didn't have them there as well, I don't even know, kind of, where I would be at this moment in time because it's been a rocky ride. They seem approachable, whereas to start with, I was quite anxious about approaching them and speaking to them, but then I gained trust in them to be able to speak to them and ask them to come and help me attend these appointments.'

Another hub user, Nicole, refers to the CSW group (that is, not just the team members but other parents) when she describes the wraparound support she has received:

'I've been coming to the hub for about a year. I think with my community, people will do a lot to help each other – if anyone is in need, people will go out their way to support you and help you with things. Just somebody to talk to. It's quite good. They've helped me immensely. I had to come out of a living situation really suddenly with nowhere to go, with nothing apart from my kids and the clothes on our backs. Without the community social work group, I don't know how I would have gotten through it. Like, helping me get into homeless accommodation and transport for getting my kids back and forward to school. They're still continuing to help me try and get into a more permanent living situation. Even just things like getting toiletries and household items just to get by. They've been really amazing every step of the way in helping. I can't thank them enough for everything.'

The team are now linked with two GP surgeries and, after detailed discussion with GPs, receive referrals directly from them, with an emphasis on relationship-based support rather than commissioned services requiring formal assessment. Sometimes, the boundaries are blurred, or become so, and this factor may lead the team in the direction of statutory referrals. This was part of the original vision and an important issue that is discussed elsewhere in this book. CSW team social workers do this already in all but name – some of the individuals being supported would merit statutory team interventions in other authorities – the Fife approach, though, is rooted in relationships and partnerships. This raises issues about the parameters of a CSW team: is their function preventative if they are a catch-all for individuals who are not getting the right services from other appropriate statutory social work or health resources? This is another question for ongoing reflection and consideration.

Fife's CSW journey continues on an uncertain course as these lines are written, and the project may not now be allocated the resources needed to continue its work and development. Changes at the senior management level are impacting, and in a climate of cuts and stringency, pragmatism might win the day, and the team's amazing work might come to an end. The authority is embarking on a service redesign involving external consultants who are looking at community-based services across departmental boundaries with a view to better working together – a direction the council has been moving in anyway through such initiatives as the one that brought the CSW team into fruition. All this creates inevitable uncertainty, especially for the staff. The example is far from perfect, and lessons have been learned along the way, with an important one being that the team should perhaps have been developed from across social work in Fife (that is, involving adult services) rather than just from a base in the children and family service. However, had this strategy been adopted, the Fife CSW initiative might never have got off the ground and offered the rich experience described in this chapter.

6

Northern Ireland: Clarendon Medical Practice's multi-disciplinary team – from 'Healthy Connections' to 'Strengthened Connections'

Introduction

The 2019 introduction of social workers into general practitioner (GP) practice-based multi-disciplinary teams (MDTs) in Northern Ireland (see Chapter 4) has resulted in a range of initiatives that might be described as community social work (CSW), though that was not necessarily their expressed purpose. The sheer variety of these is a testament to the creativity of social work staff, and this can be seen in the booklet *Social Work and Community Development* (Northern Ireland Department of Health, 2023). These vary from the Garvagh Forest Families Project, which involved families with children in a summer programme based on basic outdoor experiences with nature, to a project that reached out to Ghanaian fishermen living on vessels at the very periphery of a coastal community. These will not be retold in this chapter, but the reader is urged to look at them as a fairly unique series of contemporary CSW examples.

Clarendon Medical Practice is situated in Derry/Londonderry (hereinafter referred to as 'Derry') and, with eight GPs, offers health services to 12,000 patients across the city and its outskirts. It was among the first in the Western Trust to create an MDT in 2019 following the initial roll-out of the initiative referred to in

Chapter 4. MDT staff appointed were a physiotherapist, mental health practitioner, social worker and social work assistant (there were plans initially for 2.4 whole-time equivalent social workers, but recruitment was paused for budget reasons). What is described in this chapter shows how a health setting with an inevitable focus on health rather than social issues offers wonderful possibilities for the development of CSW. Much of the success described is down to the creativity and enthusiasm of social worker Roisin Ferry, social work assistant Caroline Stack and their manager Charmaine McNally. This narrative benefits from the fact that some of their work has been externally evaluated from a health perspective by Ulster University researcher Dr Grainne McAnee in two phases: in 2021, when the Obesity pilot evaluation was published (McAnee et al, 2021); and in 2023, with the publication of *Strengthened Connections* (McAnee, 2023).

As with so many of the examples, the drive and imagination that has brought them to fruition has centred on one or more individuals. In this case, crucially important has been Roisin Ferry – a straight-talking Derry grandmother who came into community development as a very young parent organising a playgroup involving her own children and juggling many roles at the same time as bringing up a family. After many years of youth work and community development activity, she commenced social work training at the age of 30 and spent 19 years as a children and family social worker. However, Roisin became frustrated by the lack of opportunity to do the type of social work she felt was necessary if people were to be helped to take control of their own lives.

Looking at need in a primary care setting

Roisin Ferry is now established as a senior practitioner in the Clarendon Medical Practice. She has always believed that the key to success in her role is involving individuals and families in finding their own solutions – what we now call 'co-design' and 'co-production'. As soon as she started in the Clarendon Medical Practice, she began organising meetings with staff and others to identify what was happening and what the potential was. In an echo of one of the main precepts of asset-based community development (ABCD) (Russell and McKnight, 2022), Roisin's underlying presumption from her own life experience was that the community contained many strengths and assets, not just problems that the onus was on professionals to provide solutions to resolve.

One particular issue of concern for the GPs was that, like poor communities across the UK, Derry seemed to have a high preponderance of obesity. From a social perspective, causes are associated with poor diet and lack of exercise associated with low self-esteem and hopelessness: 'Obesity is not a "choice". People become overweight or obese as a result of a complex combination of biological and psychological factors combined with environmental and social influences. Obesity is not simply put down to an individual's lack of willpower' (Perriard-Abdoh et al [2019: 9] quoted in McAnee et al [2021: 8]). These factors combine to cause chronic physical health issues that inevitably result in downstream medical interventions, as well as more immediate social issues relating to social withdrawal and loss of confidence. The GPs naturally and not inappropriately saw the MDT and its social work staff as perhaps in a position to start tackling obesity. After some initial discussion with MDT colleagues, one of the tasks suggested was for Roisin to teach patients how to shop online for healthier food. She rejected this in a forthright fashion and advised her manager that this was not the type of approach she wanted any association with; years of experience had taught her that advice on lifestyle changes and choices would fall on deaf ears unless it started by addressing underlying emotional issues, some of which were based on long-standing trauma and personal histories. Tactful persuasion enabled her to proceed on this basis.

The first task was reaching out to patients so that a process of co-design could commence. Obesity sufferers, it was found, shy away from attendance at health clinics and can be hard to reach. A start was made with a welcoming and straightforward letter from Roisin and her social work assistant colleague Caroline to all practice patients known to have a body mass index (BMI) of over 40. There were enough respondents willing to attend an initial meeting, and from them, a panel of those willing to be involved in the co-design of a programme that might help them with their issues was created. Advice was also sought from trust colleagues in health improvement, and local community groups (such as the Bogside and Brandywell Forum) were contacted with the double aim of finding potential financial and active support for the project and a source of resources and groups that could be drawn upon. The group agreed to stage a 'Dragon's Den'-style event, where a range of possible facilitators were invited to meet with the panel and tell them about their service or programme. It was agreed by the panel that the two social work staff (and researcher) would be embedded in the programme as participants in order to counteract power imbalances.

From these co-produced discussions involving patients from an early stage, the programme 'Healthy Connections' emerged, combining social activity, fun and learning with elements that addressed issues around obesity more directly in order to help participants improve their understanding of their relationship with food. This would start with an introductory session involving the MDT's mental health practitioner, who outlined a safety policy and details of support outside the group after the completion of the programme. Six weeks of sessions involved 'Taiko drumming' – a group activity combining physical activity, fun and inevitable bonding between participants. Among these sessions were 'Wellness Seeker' nights, where a local practitioner focused on emotional regulation and relationships with food. The other main sessions concerned personal development and mental well-being through activities like art and holistic therapies.

Once completed, the programme was evaluated by researcher Grainne McAnee, who, as observed already, had participated throughout. Of the 80 initial letters sent out to practice patients, 23 initially responded and 14 took part in the panel part of the process. The programme started but then suffered a delay for 12 months due to the onset of the COVID-19 pandemic. Although contact was maintained with the cohort, it was inevitable that momentum was lost and, significantly, further involvement was impacted by fears grounded in the realities of COVID-19 transmission (this was reflected in later feedback). Five individuals started the programme, and four completed it. These four were willing to provide feedback involving questionnaires and interviews, and there was a general finding that the programme had been a worthwhile exercise for all. It had impacted positively on emotional well-being, and this was translated into control over the physical aspects of the lives of those involved.

Further developments in social work in the Clarendon community: 'Strengthened Connections'

Despite setbacks caused by the COVID-19 pandemic, the benefits to patients involved in the Healthy Connections pilot were clear to other partners, including the Clarendon Medical Practice GPs. Roisin and Caroline had opened up connections with others in the community and were keen to extend this style of working alongside them. The aim was to create a 'community of wellness' centred on the Clarendon Medical Practice and based on the notion of 'health precincts', as discussed by Oprescu et al (2023, cited in McAnee, 2023). Impetus was given to the idea through the successful collaborations achieved in Healthy Connections, and this resulted in the formation of Yellow Wood Consultancy, a limited company composed of those who delivered aspects of the programme. This was set up to access funding to deliver more of this type of service in the community, initially through the Ideas Fund – a grants programme established by the London-based British Science Association to 'develop and try out ideas that address problems related to mental wellbeing by working with researchers' (Ideas Fund, nd). This time, a fresh Strengthened Connections group would be aimed at any patients from the Clarendon Medical Practice who wanted to participate in a well-being programme aimed at improving mental health. The 28 who were selected and recruited by the social work staff (in consultation with GPs) had a variety of backgrounds and experiences: some had addiction issues; some were carers under great stress; some were suffering from work-related stress and burnout; some were very socially isolated; and some had suffered many years of mental ill health. Entering a group with others not known to them was a daunting experience for many, but as with Healthy Connections, Roisin and Caroline were always there to ensure inclusivity and sensitivity, and they could react quickly to signs of individual need. As has been the experience elsewhere of social workers undertaking CSW, some participants were initially weary about the social workers' motives for being present but, according to the evaluation conducted later, were quickly won over to their role as caring professionals willing to work alongside them through the course of the programme.

The Strengthened Connections programme itself was designed to take place over a six-week period. It involved much of the same type of activity as Healthy Connections and centred around the well-being contributions of the Yellow Wood presenters. Week 1 was an introductory session, where the concepts underlying a safe, inclusive and supportive space were explained; Week 2 used a medium of cards with symbolic meanings, which enabled group members to become more aware of their own strengths, qualities and values; Week 3 utilised a vision board to continue the theme of self-awareness and self-support; Week 4's session taught participants basic emotional freedom techniques (EFTs); in Week 5, they were all invited to bring along an object that was meaningful to them and share it with the group; the finale in Week 6 involved each person being presented with a treasure box symbolising what they should take away from the experiences of the previous six weeks and use as tools for future well-being.

Follow-up quantitative and qualitative research demonstrated that participants came out of the group with enhanced feelings of well-being and motivation. Using a tried-and-tested system for mental well-being (the Warwick Edinburgh Mental Wellbeing Scale, which operates on a scale from 14 at the lower end to 70 at the higher end), mean scores were raised from 40 (with wide variation) to 49 (with less variation). The hosting GPs are reported to be very pleased with the work promoted through their MDT social work staff, stating in the formal evaluation document that they feel their practice now cares for its community, as well as treating their medical disorders.

An important message for participants in Strengthened Connections was that their individual journeys should continue through activities led and facilitated by group members as well as Yellow Wood and the social work staff from the practice: other initiatives were agreed and co-produced with participants, to which other practice patients have been invited to become involved. Peer mentors giving of their time for free were identified from the initial Healthy Connections cohort and others through Yellow Wood and the social work staff who have encouraged and led activity. A Patients Committee has been formed from 13 interested individuals, including all four of the Healthy Connections group. This committee is now applying for funding to work on issues they have identified in the community and coordinate all the groups and activities that have mushroomed through Healthy Connections and the work that followed.

One activity that has gone from strength to strength is the Clarendon Medical Practice Community Allotment, which evolved from Healthy Connections: at the time of the 2023 evaluation, 33 patients were noted to have become involved. The initial idea came from Grainne, the researcher who had heard of similar initiatives elsewhere. The allotment site was identified by the social work staff in a park area of Derry, 'Playtrail', which they had used to maintain outdoor contact with the Healthy Connections cohort through the pandemic-enforced social distancing. The small rent is paid for by the Clarendon Medical Practice. Roisin has used some of her seed funding to facilitate work in the allotment and has applied successfully for other grants to enable development to continue. This includes an award won at a Belfast 'Dragons Den' event, which paid for patient training, music therapy, hypnotherapy and coaching/mentoring.

A leading figure in the allotment is one of the original four from the Healthy Connections group, who is also now a leading light on the Patients Committee, and another key contributor has emerged from the Strengthened Connections activity. Activities have sprouted around this to broaden collective and cooperative involvement and to place the allotment, and its output of fresh fruit and vegetables, at the heart of community efforts to address cost-of-living issues for residents in the area.

Another aspect of patient activity that has brightened up the area around the surgery is the photographic exhibition of work by the ten patients who took part in a photography course organised and funded by Yellow Wood. Other patients now lead a walking group – the 'Clarendon Danders' – which had 33 members in early 2023. A Taiko drumming group has been formed following its introduction as part of the Healthy Connections programme, with ten members. Additionally, 'music for wellbeing workshops' have been held, so far involving 40 patients. One of the peer mentors has started two-hour 'intuitive art' workshops, with 20 patients attending early sessions. One peer mentor organised a family day centred on the allotment, and another peer facilitated an introduction to crystal meditation workshop. Activities are promoted by Roisin and Caroline through the Clarendon Medical Practice's social media Facebook page and a YouTube Channel started by Yellow Wood, with contributions from community members.

The social work staff continue to support individuals: as a direct result of their involvement in Healthy Connections and Strengthened Connections, Roisin has set aside some time for one-to-one anxiety management work with patients. She and Caroline have also undertaken specialised training in the delivery of regular 'emotional eating workshops' for practice patients. The researcher, Grainne McAnee, advised the author that the social work staff have been central to developments, and it is unlikely any of the progress made would have been possible without their deployment to the MDT and their creative approach to developing the Clarendon community. Their role as community social workers is understated in the two published evaluations, rich as they are in recorded oral testimony from users and data concerning outcomes. This is because the focus of the evaluations was slanted towards the mental well-being requirements of the Ideas Fund, which, through the Yellow Wood Consultancy, has been a crucially important funder of the community projects and groups.

Yellow Wood produced a short video, 'Noma's Story', where one of the actively involved patients describes her journey from arrival as a refugee in Derry, with communication, social isolation and many other issues, to her role now as a confident peer mentor and Patients Committee member. She talks of how Roisin and Caroline helped her with personal issues and how, through the groups and activities they introduced her to, she now volunteers and helps others. This is a lasting testament to the power and potential of CSW.

The experience of the Clarendon Medical Practice MDT social worker and social work assistant demonstrates CSW in practice. Their work has been founded on a belief that co-design and co-production are effective means to help people reshape their lives positively. The combination of creativity, outward-looking networking and community development expertise, alongside social work skill in relationships, has resulted in outcomes that would not have been imaginable using traditional individual casework approaches to the needs of the community concerned – patients of a large GP practice.

7

Wales: examples of community orientation and community social work from Carmarthenshire and Torfaen

Introduction

This chapter offers two examples from practice. The first example, from Carmarthenshire, describes the community orientation of a substance misuse team in addressing issues arising from alcohol-related brain damage (ARBD). This has used imaginative approaches and community resources to transcend clinical and referral boundaries and provide a service that can demonstrate positive outcomes. The narrative includes the words of an individual service user who tells his own story of the benefits of such approaches.

The second example looks at the practice of a statutory adult team (known as a wellbeing team) in Torfaen. Here, they changed their approach to adult care a number of years ago, replacing a centralised service, use of eligibility criteria and standard assessment-based methods, with a neighbourhood-based service approach. The result has been an eradication of waiting lists, an increase in satisfaction reported by staff, users and carers and a reduction of commissioned services in favour of individualised preventative upstream solutions based on extensive knowledge of the community and networking.

Example 1: The Carmarthenshire Substance Misuse Team

Gary James is the team manager of the small Carmarthenshire Substance Misuse Team, with just five social workers covering the whole county from a base in Llanelli. With a background in design but a 20-year career in social work, he has always, he says, sought to find ways to be creative in his practice. The team he leads have been innovative and creative, to the extent that the story of their work with sufferers of alcohol-related brain damage (ARBD) provides a useful illustration, not of CSW, which is not their purpose or design, but of community orientation by a team committed to finding ways to be more effective than traditional prescribed routes seem to permit. Gary is described by one of his workers, Rebecca Phillips, 'Becs' as she is known, as someone "not interested in stats and things like that and always getting [into] rows for breaking rules". However, without Gary's drive and vision and permission for staff to find new and different solutions to issues, it is unlikely that the ARBD project would have happened. As a beacon of good practice, the team have been joined by equally committed workers, including Becs, whose account as the team's senior practitioner of their work and her own journey is included in this example. It has also filled vacancies with students who have enjoyed placements with the team – a practice that is encouraged, with most of the social workers now trained up to offer placements.

Gary explains that the 'Prochaska and DiClemente model' of the change cycle commonly adopted by substance misuse workers and teams did not fit the ARBD client group, who were stuck in the pre-contemplation stage (Prochaska and DiClemente, 1983). As it was accepted practice that informed consent was required for referral acceptance and that the absence of this precluded offering a service, Gary was conscious that a growing number of referrals from the police and others represented needs that were largely going unmet. In his view, an imaginative approach was required to get around the rules and provide a service to meet rising demand (an example of the positive use of discretion described by Lipsky [1980] and referred to in Chapter 2). Demand rose because of the social isolation compounded by the COVID-19 pandemic. While informed consent is often used to screen out referrals when this is not forthcoming, Gary's approach was to quote adult protection and safeguarding legislation to challenge this assumption and offer help, sometimes persistently until it was taken up and real work commenced.

Using sustained relationship-based social work and motivational interviewing techniques, combined with knowledge and use of local resources and networks, Gary soon proved that it was possible to achieve success and has since been able to secure additional Welsh government funding via the Area Planning Board (a multi-agency coordinating group for substance misuse work covering Carmarthenshire and its two neighbouring counties). His staff working with ARBD sufferers worked closely with the domiciliary care workers who were deployed to provide practical support: their skills and knowledge as local people to their service users were very important. The team now have two 'recovery practitioners': former domiciliary carers who provide practical support alongside social workers, whose own relationship-based interventions are often part of the care plan. The importance of domiciliary care as a component of recovery has been recognised to the extent that the council are now considering taking services back in-house so that consistent and managed services can operate effectively.

The team's interventions have resulted in brain damage through alcohol use being reversed: several individuals whose lives were on a downward spiral have been helped to recover to the point that a service was no longer required. The staff are encouraged to walk alongside people and use their own time and skills rather than assess and refer on to others; this is appreciated by service users, who feel that they are known as individuals, cared for and respected as people.

The value of the team's approach can be seen through the account given by one of Becs' service users:

> 'Two years ago, I was in a mess: I wasn't washing myself, my flat was a tip and I was getting into bother with other people. I was drinking every day to oblivion. I was using the food bank. I wasn't

managing my medication or my money. I was ignoring letters and not answering the door to people. I was punishing myself.

My life started to change when Becs came on the scene; I was in a bad way and she listened to me. She started to sort stuff out for me. She respected me. She did the things she said she was going to do. She matched me with carers who got on with me – people with patience that lifted my spirits. She helped me to identify my own strengths, and it's taken me 60-odd years to do it, but I think I know the real me now. I don't want to die anymore.

I get out of bed in a flat that I love and feel settled in. From when I wake up, I am doing my best to get into a routine. I have pride in my flat and myself. I have started going to a cookery group and doing my own shopping. I've had help to budget: I can go to shop now and not have to worry about how much I spend, as I know I have savings for the first time in my life.

I feel really safe. I can go over past memories without the same level of hurt. My body isn't as tense now; I genuinely feel relaxed. I can laugh about things. I am sleeping. I do feel guilty, though, for having a lovely home, a full freezer; it's almost like it's not mine.'

As well as individual work, team members use unstructured group working: Becs invited a number of service users to walk with her in a group and used the time to talk to them individually. They now use an established walking group for the same purpose. On other occasions, she has organised minibus trips and coffee mornings. Structured groupwork is also deployed, for example, around relapse prevention, and both types of approach have resulted in peer-run groups and activities.

Becs Phillips: a worker's own journey

Becs qualified in 2011 and worked initially in a mental health team. She then took time off to have children and returned to a community care team because work was offered on a part-time basis, which suited her family commitments. However, she found the care management model in operation quite unrewarding and deskilling: people referred were offered an initial assessment, and service was reviewed after six weeks and the social worker withdrawn from further involvement. This offered no opportunity to work with people in a relational way. To work her way into something better, Becs took advantage of every training opportunity she could, and on one of these, she listened to Gary present his team's approach to ARBD. With her background in mental health, Becs realised that this was the sort of social work she wanted to practise, and as soon as a vacancy came up, she applied – that was four years ago. She now works full-time and is the team's senior practitioner.

Becs has helped introduce a collective approach to referrals that come to the team: meetings take place with others involved, and care plans are devised based on long and detailed assessment based on the individual's own story rather than the labels they come with. Allocation is determined at weekly team meetings through what she describes as a 'pod' system, where workers are mutually supportive and share ideas. The workers all bring different skills and experiences to the team, and these are used to the full in determining allocation. As said earlier, the key to the team's approach is based on sustained and personal involvement by the allocated social worker, which Becs describes as 'detective'-like: piecing things together over time alongside the service user and being with them on this part of their journey.

Local knowledge and networking are important attributes. Becs herself is from Llanelli, where much of the team's work is located because it is the main population centre. She knows people from as far back as her own time at local schools and understands their networks and backgrounds. Living and working in the same place presents challenges, but she can walk with her children through the town centre at weekends, where street drinkers and homeless people whom she knows through work are present, and finds that she is always treated respectfully and appropriately. Becs is generally fulfilled by her work and continuing to take advantage of additional training, with the support of Gary and more senior managers; she is currently completing a team management course through Oxford Brookes University.

Gary and Becs both testify that the team they work with are proud of their approach and pleased that their efforts are recognised and valued by senior management in their authority. Most rewarding, though, is the feeling that outcomes are positive for the individuals they are supporting.

Example 2: The Blaenavon adult care team, Torfaen

Torfaen is a small local authority area in South Wales, with its geography centred around a broad valley running for 13 miles from the new town of Cwmbran through the main town of Pontypool and on to the old mining and industrial area of Blaenavon. The county borough has a population of just over 93,000, 6,000 of whom live in Blaenavon and its immediate environs. Blaenavon, the area under focus here, has a proud history of iron making and coal mining going back to the start of the Industrial Revolution. Nowadays, the economy of the town rests on heritage and small industrial concerns. While its population is ageing, there are still young people in the community, but endemic poverty and its symptoms, such as drug misuse and anti-social behaviour, are persistent features.

The redesign of adult care services

In 2015, the council, encouraged by enlightened senior managers who had an eye on developments in the neighbouring authority of Monmouthshire, decided to embark on a root-and-branch review of adult social services. This was also inspired by the new Social Services and Well-Being Act (see Chapter 4), with its emphasis on prevention, early intervention and the co-production of services. Until then, services in Torfaen had developed along siloed, centralised lines, with separate teams delivering parallel services across the county to different adult user groups. These rested on an eligibility-defined care management model, with service users being passed between staff from different teams and constantly having to retell their stories in order to receive a specific service. This was described by a manager as "transactional and tick-box", offering little opportunity for continuity or relationship-based work. It was unpopular with users and carers, and staff morale was low.

With the help of external consultants (Vanguard Consultancy), a review was undertaken that comprised a six-day intensive session involving consultation with users and carers. This resulted in a decision made that there would be a return to four 'patch-based' teams (the very 1980s' term used in Torfaen). This was later extended to five teams. This model would replace the plethora of duty and specialised teams that had existed until that point (except for learning disability and adult mental health because of their enmeshment with health services). It was decided that this would start with a pilot in Blaenavon led by an experienced manager, Sam Jones, whose experience went back to the community orientation that was taken for granted at the time she trained and first came into social work. Her team of eight social workers and assistants included Alison Lawson-Jones, who was equally keen to get back to a relationship- and community-based working model.

In a similar style to the Fife initiative described in Chapter 5, the team started in Blaenavon, with no caseloads carried through from their previous teams. Picking up new referrals they termed 'Job 1', and one referral was taken on in the earliest days. This left plenty of time for 'Job 2', which was to get to know their locality as a community and start talking to other agencies and local people about the type of service they wanted for adults and older people in need. This involved multiple conversations and simply walking around finding out where the shops and other community resources were, as well as how they operated. Discussions among themselves led to the drafting of nine principles, which have remained fundamental to the team's approach since:

1. Listen to, understand what matters – don't just give what we have got.
2. Build on people's own strengths, networks and community.
3. Design work against predictable demand.
4. Expertise upfront.
5. Pull in, don't refer or 'hand-off' [that is, pass on to other teams].

6. Only do value work.
7. Proportionate, purposeful, person-centred recording.
8. Proportionate, purposeful, person-centred practice.
9. Never say never, problem solve and unblock.

The new service involved an open-door, no-duty system, and services provided were based on a hierarchy of support, which was determined through close involvement by staff with the person concerned and holistic knowledge of their life and circumstances. When discussing this with Sam and Alison, I asked what the pathway might be if I was a stressed-out carer caring for an elderly person with no services and looking for a break. According to the old model, an assessment for respite would be undertaken and respite probably then provided through a commissioned service. Under the new model, the social worker might offer a break in the first instance by providing some of their own time to spend with the elderly person and then use this to really get to know them and their world. What was often realised was that solutions to presenting issues could be found through local resources that might be provided informally through community organisations, neighbours or other family members. The commissioned service would come at the end of the process, and what the team have found is that through their approach, this is often not required.

The reviewing process is seen not as a single moment but as an ongoing process, so interventions and services evolve; statutory meetings take place as required but tend to produce no surprises. Recording is proportionate, as is the use of computerised assessment paperwork; the emphasis in the team was described as 'sofas, not computers' – workers should spend time with the people being supported, not in the office caught up with remote systems that make little difference to outcomes.

The team have found that through their open-door approach and after six years or so of operation, they now know their community to the extent that issues are headed off at an early stage: less crisis and demands that are met without either waiting lists or eligibility criteria. The care management model has been replaced by a relationship-based service centred on early intervention, good networking and local knowledge. No longer is there any need for an emphasis on screening people out; instead, ongoing contact and return are welcomed.

Working in the Torfaen adult care team

What struck me when talking to Sam and Alison was the extent to which their team are stable and happy in their work, with little staff turnover. They came out of COVID-19 restrictions as quickly as they could and returned to their team office base as the centre of their practice world. This is co-located with health colleagues, with relationships with National Health Service (NHS) staff determined by networking and working together at the front-line level rather than formal top-down protocols. Workers have their own office space and use each other's experiences and knowledge freely; collective learning is considered important. Each working day starts with a 'fishbowl' meeting. This concept is central to team functioning, and a document they prepared to explain it to others describes it as follows:

> The fishbowl is a daily, strengths based, reflective session that is mandatory for the whole team to participate in. The team are disciplined, in that it happens every morning at 9.30 and has a particular structure to allow reflection and challenge. This is to ensure that we have stuck to our principles and to the hierarchy of support when looking for possible solutions – which is the person's own past or current networks, then community services and lastly commissioned services. The worker who has visited talks about the person with a strengths based, person centred focus without interruption for a maximum of 15 mins. The team then ask clarification questions and then the team reach a solution, challenging to ensure we have stuck to principles and the hierarchy of support. The discussion is recorded to show evidence of reflection and decision making. It acts as a group supervision and is derived from participative democracy, shared decision making.

These often involve developing ideas through means like flipcharts, and the nine principles are constantly referred to as a baseline. Workers get regular sessions of 'one-to-one support' (a term used instead of 'supervision') from their particular manager (the team has a manager, Sam, and two assistant managers, including Alison). Language is considered important, and an early decision was made to identify themselves as the 'North Torfaen Wellbeing Team'. Caseloads are manageable, and allocation is made on the basis of mutual agreement, with workers typically volunteering to take on a new referral. As there is no formal duty system, everyone takes phone calls concerning new referrals if they are in the office; this works well and often marks the start of worker continuity. Later inquiries from individuals whose services have ended are welcomed, and workers are flattered (Rather than concerned!) if they are asked for by name. Contrary to some expectations, this style has not resulted in over-dependency and such issues are managed quite adequately by staff as part of their whole relationship-based approach to community need.

The team in the community and feedback

While much of the team's strength lies in its informal networking, open-door policy and local knowledge, it has also helped improve more formal local resource coordination. A Healthy Blaenavon group brings together numerous statutory and third sector agencies, local politicians, community businesses, and others. A Neighbourhood Community Network is more focused on health issues. Good working relationships are maintained with a social housing provider, the Bron Afon Housing Association.

The progress made with the patch-based system has been partially recognised by the Wales Care Inspectorate through their formal inspection of adult services in Torfaen in October 2019, and to them will go the last word, for most of the county borough change was at an early stage, and the inspection did not differentiate between Torfaen (then, three years in) and the other four patches. As might be expected, the report did have some issues with service delivery, but in general, it was welcoming and reflected what service users and carers told inspectors:

Torfaen CBC's [County Borough Council] vision for patch-based teams was developed in collaboration with service users. We heard from an individual how the team 'enables me to live my life the way I choose to live it'. [Patch-based] teams are now having very different conversations with people focusing on what matters to them, their wider wellbeing and not solely on service eligibility. People we met felt clearly involved. We found some assessments capturing the individual goals and objectives in the person's own words, clearly evidencing what matters conversation taking place. There is a commitment to further improve the skills of staff in this area with training for all in collaborative communication and motivational conversations. (Wales Care Inspectorate, 2019: 12)

As well as involvement in the internal training of staff for the patch system model, the Blaenavon team is held up as an exemplar by Torfaen Social Services, often hosting visitors keen to see how they operate, including from the Welsh government.

8

Community social work with a marginalised minority ethnic group: Gypsy and Traveller communities in England

Introduction

While the Black Lives Matter movement that originated in the US has brought about a welcome focus on the lasting impact of slavery and helped progress the postcolonial narrative as a cornerstone of social work with people of colour, this has barely touched the UK's oldest minority ethnic group: Gypsy, Romani and Travellers (the preferred term rather than the convenient abbreviation 'GRT', which fails to describe quite distinct cultures and backgrounds), as well as associated groups facing similar issues: Boaters, Show People and New Age Travellers.

A recent study on social work with Gypsy, Romani and Traveller children in the state system found pejorative and ill-informed attitudes, as well as oppressive actions that flowed from them (Allen and Riding, 2018). This triggered a further study that discussed the concept of 'aversive racism'; this, the authors argue, is found among social workers who will claim to be non-discriminatory and to support notions of equal opportunity but nonetheless harbour prejudices (Allen and Hulmes, 2021). This results in practice with Gypsy, Romani and Travellers that fails to take account of culture and custom, seeing safeguarding issues where there are none and basing decisions on false premises.

Out of such work grew the Gypsy, Roma and Traveller Social Work Association (GRTSWA), established through the British Association of Social Workers (BASW) in 2019/20, with the aim of improving communication and understanding and breaking down barriers between social workers and Travelling communities. The BASW (2022) consequently published a statement on anti-Gypsyism and Gypsy, Romani and Traveller rights.

This chapter will look at the work of one individual, Wiltshire County Council social worker Chris Kidd, who applies his GRTSWA knowledge and commitment through both his work as a children's safeguarding social worker for his local authority and his role as lead for their Traveller Reference Group (TRG). The chapter therefore focuses not on a geographical community but on one based on ethnic identity and culture, spread across a large area and sharing issues with others throughout the UK. The chapter will also cover the essence of good practice with this community in a more general way.

Gypsies, Roma people and Travellers

It is difficult to briefly summarise the extent of prejudice, both institutional and otherwise, that is commonly experienced by the UK's Travelling communities. The origins of discrimination lie in the historical marginalisation of the Gypsy people, who arrived in the UK hundreds of years ago, having journeyed over time from the Indian sub-continent, bringing with them a distinct culture and nomadic way of life that has almost always been under direct and indirect assault by the settled community and its institutions. Such prejudice has been extended over the last few centuries to nomadic peoples whose ethnic origins might differ but whose experiences are shaped by suspicion and misunderstanding from mainstream communities. This is not unique to the UK: Roma communities elsewhere in Europe face routine discrimination and violence (up to half a million were murdered by the Nazis in the Second World War's Holocaust), causing many in recent years to move to the UK through their European Union citizenship – a pathway now closed. They too have encountered hostility in the UK. Racism against these communities takes many forms, including:

- Negative stereotyping of Gypsy, Romani and Traveller community members.
- Intolerance of Gypsy, Romani and Traveller community members as neighbours.
- Official policies that force assimilation into mainstream society.
- A dearth of culturally sensitive public services. (Cemlyn et al, 2009)

These all combine to perpetuate health inequalities and a shortened life expectancy (Hulmes and Unwin, forthcoming). Gypsy and Traveller communities are found throughout the UK, and most individual families (up to 75 per cent) are settled in houses or on permanent caravan sites but take their culture and identity with them (Hulmes and Unwin, forthcoming). Changes in the economy that have rendered itinerant working a difficult choice, as well as a dearth of stopover possibilities, have combined to force many Travellers to curtail their traditional mode of life, and some have felt forced to hide their ancestry so as not to attract discrimination. Recent research from England suggests that Gypsies and Travellers are more likely than other communities to have their children removed into state care – a fear based on folk memory as well as modern-day experience that impacts on willingness to engage with services (Allen and Hamnett, 2022).

These communities are likely to experience hate crime, which is known to have a 'ripple effect' on individuals, resulting in mental health problems and a high prevalence of suicide (Greenfields and Rogers, 2020). The study by Greenfields and Rogers (2020), conducted over a six-year period, found that the principal Gypsy, Roma and Traveller communities reported that within the previous five years, suicide attempts by respondents' relatives had been experienced by 100 per cent of Welsh Gypsies, 80 per cent of Scottish Gypsy Travellers, 82 per cent of Irish Travellers and 32 per cent of Romani Gypsies (a lower but still frightening figure).

Minority ethnic status in terms of the Equality Act 2010 has applicability throughout the UK and affords protected characteristics and (previously afforded) minority ethnic status to English Gypsies, Welsh Gypsies, Irish Travellers and Scottish Gypsy Travellers. However, other modern legislation, such as the Police, Crime, Sentencing and Courts Act 2022, has tightened up trespass laws for England and Wales and rendered a nomadic lifestyle more problematic, criminalising individuals and families caught up in the new system. The number of local authority sites for Travelling communities has also reduced, and the majority of caravan dwellers in England (estimated to be 71 per cent of a total of 23,000 people) are now on privately owned land with varying degrees of security (Ministry of Housing, Communities and Local Government, 2020).

Working with Gypsy Travellers and Travelling communities: Chris Kidd

Chris qualified as a social worker in 2019 and, prior to professional training, worked for 20 years as a youth worker, where he developed an interest in Gypsy Travellers and gained experience through working alongside community members in several locations across the South of England. This included a period as an outreach worker in Essex, where he worked with residents in Dale Farm. He chose the Gypsy, Romani and Traveller communities as the subject of his final master's dissertation.

Dale Farm came to national attention when the residents were served with eviction notices despite long residence and regular use of the land, as well as legal ownership by some residents. The site lay adjacent to an official site run by Basildon Council. The legal battle went on for ten years, highlighting many issues, including local and national prejudices and mistrust inflamed by tabloid newspapers, as well as differences over a long period between English Romani Gypsies and the Irish Travellers who predominated on the site during the period of the legal battle. The council's argument, backed by many neighbouring community residents, was that they were not prepared to give planning permission for this additional site in a designated 'Green Belt' area. The residents argued not only that this was a traditional stopping place but also that the council that wanted them off the land had used it as a dumping ground for unwanted tarmac and other materials for many years. By 2011, as the legal process was falling in favour of the council, an international group of human rights monitors, Camp Constant, was on site, supported by the residents. The United Nations Commissioner for Human Rights became involved and attempted to mediate, but this was rejected by the Foreign Office. Eventually, a violent confrontation involving residents and their supporters (including many local people) and about 100 riot police occurred on 19 October 2011, when 200 bailiffs arrived to evict an expected 400 residents, including 100 children. The eviction went ahead, the residents dispersed and the buildings and infrastructure of the community were torn down by contractors, much of it remaining for many years just as it was left by the bailiffs and their demolition crew (*The Guardian*, 2011, 2021). Curiosity about the Traveller lifestyle on the back of publicity through the years of the Dale Farm eviction process spawned a TV series, Big Fat Gypsy Weddings, regarded as pejorative and misleading by many in the communities whose lives it was said to portray. It was also said to have increased anti-Gypsy racism and the bullying of young people (*The Guardian*, 2012).

Chris's experience with Dale Farm and his witness to what happened there have shaped his involvement with the community since, though have also granted him access to families generally mistrustful of officials that might otherwise have been difficult. Chris, along with Jackie Bolton (an independent social worker in Essex who is herself a Romani Gypsy), Alison Hulmes (a social worker who is a Welsh Kale Gypsy), Dan Allen (whose academic work was quoted earlier) and others, helped set up the GRTSWA in 2019/20.

The GRTSWA has published a good practice guide based on issues arising from the Police, Crime, Sentencing and Courts Act 2022 (Allen and GRTSWA, 2022). This guide tries to address issues for the estimated 10,000 families who, under this legislation, will have no safe and secure stopping place in England and Wales (Friends, Families and Travellers, 2020). Importantly, the guide provides a two-part template for conducting a welfare enquiry that can be used to support those adversely affected by the legislation and facing police action. This will help social workers (and others) ask the right questions about a family's or individual's circumstances and why they came to be in the place from which they are being forcibly removed.

The children's safeguarding team to which Chris belongs can find themselves at the heart of official concerns about Gypsy, Romani and Traveller families in their area of Wiltshire. As noted earlier, it is sadly not unusual for 'aversive racist' misunderstandings about families to result in confrontation and oppressive reactions. If a family is referred for an enquiry, Chris does not necessarily respond personally but will help guide his colleagues and aid their assessments. In this way, others are educated, assumptions are challenged and attitudes are changed. The model welfare assessments referred to earlier have been used in cases involving actions under the Police, Crime and Sentencing Act 2022.

Due to his interest in these communities, Chris became involved with Wiltshire Council's TRG, initially as a contributor but currently leading this multi-agency body, representing a significant step forward for social work influence in its workings. This brings together housing, communications, commissioning, planning, enforcement, early help public health, community engagement, councillor representation and external partner representatives from health, police and fire services. The TRG was set up following the publication of the council's 'Traveller Strategy' in 2010, refreshed in 2016 and substantially updated in 2020 by Public Health Registrar Dr Michael Allum (2020), who incorporated a health strategy focused on the county's Boater population. The group meets four times a year with the task of overseeing the implementation of the priorities identified in the strategy, with the overarching ones being education attainment and attendance, preventative services, safeguarding and violence prevention, and mental health. These all involve some culturally sensitive activities, awareness raising and information gathering, conducted in partnership with members of the communities concerned and involving such organisations as Friends, Families and Travellers (a Traveller-led charity). Chris has personally been involved in awareness training delivered to over 1,000 Wiltshire Council staff.

The Wiltshire TRG has hosted drop-in sessions at the three official Traveller sites in Wiltshire and taken up issues raised by residents. It has also sponsored awareness-raising projects, with an example being Gypsy Traveller History Month in June 2023, involving schools and libraries. During the COVID-19 pandemic, following on from the work undertaken in 2019, the group initiated a floating vaccination resource, sponsored with neighbouring authorities, which visited the Boater communities along the Kennet and Avon Canal. The TRG, on Chris's initiative, is also looking at the possibility of introducing the idea of 'sanctuary stopping places' in Wiltshire: safe and legal site provision for Travelling communities to use, an idea started by the Gypsy Traveller-led organisation LeedsGATE as an answer to the issues created by the 2022 legislation. Sanctuary stopping would involve the local authority providing water, toilets and refuse collection, as well as signposting to health and welfare support, and could possibly work in Wiltshire.

Chris has co-written a chapter in a recent book on adult social work practice with three members of the Gypsy, Romani and Traveller communities, which looks at how social work practice might be improved and anti-oppressive and anti-discriminatory practice might be embodied (Kidd, 2023). This is based on experiences in Wiltshire. It particularly looks at how the welfare provisions of the Care Act 2014 can be used positively and how definitions of eligibility and normal residence can be applied regardless of a travelling way of life. Tips are offered from conversations with other members of the GRTSWA:

- Those from GTR communities often have a strong preference for carers from within their own community.
- Many GTR carers would not identify themselves as 'carers' and may not be aware that they themselves can receive support ... [and may not] access support if they do not feel the service being offered is culturally appropriate.
- Those from GTR communities may have strong preferences around the gender of the person caring for them, especially if intimate care is required.
- Those from GTR communities can have limited literacy skills but may be reluctant to admit this leading to an inability to fill in forms.
- Do not underestimate the psychological distress and unfamiliarity for those from nomadic communities placed inside bricks and mortar for hospital and palliative care. (Kidd, 2023: 89–90)

Among other very useful information is advice about Gypsy and Traveller norms regarding cleanliness and hygiene.

Without taking credit away from his colleagues in Wiltshire, there seems little doubt that Chris Kidd has used his learned skills and experience to improve social work practice among the Gypsy, Romani and Traveller communities in the area and positively influenced other public sector bodies. His work also provides useful examples of co-production to address individual situations of need and improve the lives of those in the communities in general.

9

Learning from contemporary experience: reflections on the examples from across the UK

Introduction

Chapters 5–8 have offered five very different examples of practice from Scotland, Northern Ireland, Wales and England. This chapter will look at what they can tell us about what is happening on the ground and what the potential might be for further developments of community social work (CSW), as well as, given the separation made in this book, how they might encourage community-orientated practice. It looks at commonalities, that is, factors found across the board that might be considered crucial to such developments, as well as others that mark out difference, with some explanation about why they might have emerged. This includes funding mechanisms and their effect on sustainability.

Common factors for creating CSW

The first thing that might strike the reader of Chapters 5–8 is that although the five initiatives or examples of practice that are described fit with policy in their respective nations (see later), all were the result of individual inspiration that was picked up by others and carried forward. The individuals involved, whether they were initial drivers or joiners, would all subscribe to values of social justice and a wish to make the communities they work in better places than they found them. All were, to various degrees, unhappy with the models of service delivery that have become embedded in practice: care management and models concerned mainly with risk. In Fife, Torfaen and Carmarthenshire, the bureaucratic requirements of employing organisations have been adapted and reworked so that they are a means rather than an end in themselves. It is refreshing to find that individuals willing to stand up to and challenge accepted but quite obviously flawed orthodoxies can be found at all levels within organisations responsible for statutory service – from the front line to senior management (the Leeds and Northumbria models of assessment mentioned in Chapter 3 offer imaginative ways forward even if not part of a CSW model). The workers in all the settings described are proud of what they do and care very much for their communities and the people they work alongside. Specific mention was made of visionary leadership in the Fife example, but it was found in them all to one extent or another, and it is worth noting from Chapter 1 that changes in management and personnel contributed to the ending of some of the projects of the 1970s and 1980s – a factor emerging in Fife as this book was being completed.

Another common denominator was the actuality of co-design and co-production in all the examples, as well as the manner in which this promoted policy had been embraced and made real as a concept. This was found: in Fife and Torfaen, with the model used to develop services; in Derry, where they have taken it a stage further and nurtured peer mentors; in Carmarthenshire, where recovered alcohol-related brain damage (ARBD) sufferers are now helping others with the same issue; and in Wiltshire, where real effort has been made to listen to and recruit the help of communities, used to combat deference and prejudice.

On this last point, feedback from service users reported in these chapters has often included comments expressing surprise at the helpful and supportive role of social workers. This generally resonates with research findings indicating that while people are often weary about social work involvement in their lives, actual experience can be positive (Dawson, 2020; McCulloch and Webb, 2020). This lends support to the idea that social workers are at their best when involved directly in interventions with people rather than engaging in brief assessments and handovers to other services.

A feature found in all the examples were attempts, not always very conscious ones, to reimagine the language used around services offered (an issue discussed in Chapter 3). In community models that see service users as partners and co-creators of services, language that signifies an 'us' and 'them' attitude is naturally set aside for that which embodies the warmth of relationship-based services. In Blaenavon, the team now call themselves the 'North Torfaen Wellbeing Team' and, with a model of collective daily decision making (the 'fishbowl'), have renamed supervision sessions between staff and managers as 'one-to-one support'. In Carmarthenshire, social worker Becs Phillips commented to the author that the title 'Substance Misuse Team' was perhaps unhelpful in explaining their task and purpose and that a better one was needed. Their collective method of allocation is known as the 'pod'.

As with language, the challenge to notions of professionalism finds an echo in other developing practices (also discussed in Chapter 3). In Fife, while the office base is used by staff to catch up, do administrative tasks and support one another in various ways, all their work with people is undertaken out in the community and in people's homes if enhanced support is being provided. The idea of 'office appointments' and office-based 'interviews' (as denoting professional distance and defined territory) has been discarded entirely. If a neutral venue is needed for a one-to-one chat session, there are discreet facilities in the community that can be used.

All the examples also demonstrate the creativity and artistry discussed in Chapters 2 and 3. In Carmarthenshire, Gary, the team manager, was especially proud of this factor and consciously acknowledged and encouraged it among his staff. In Fife, it was facilitated through the proposal forms completed by those with ideas and discussed collectively. In Torfaen, this was part of the daily 'fishbowl' meeting process. In Derry, this lay behind the creation of Yellow Wood and other developments, such as the Patients Committee. While the role of the social workers was discreet, the evaluations point to their central role in driving and facilitating the generation of new ideas and supporting their implementation. This is also seen among front-line staff: the contributions to this book of Molly Crombie in Fife and Becs Phillips in Carmarthenshire both evidence creativity and artistry. What was also commonly found was the willingness and enthusiasm staff shared to go out and talk to others about their experiences, whether through workshops at conferences (Fife and Derry), talks to university students (Fife), training (Torfaen, Wiltshire and Carmarthenshire) or even a national conference devoted to CSW that involved service users (Fife).

One observation of the two CSW examples is that in neither case did preparation involve an examination of evidence from the 1980s, or of literature from that period (for example, Hadley et al's [1987] handbook), when these models were last tried. Perhaps they are so far back and the literature so dated and hard to find that this seemed of little relevance. Hopefully, the examples brought back to life in Chapter 1 can be put to good use.

Fitting with official policy

Official policies for social welfare matters tend not to be prescriptive and therefore open areas of opportunity for development, as discussed in Chapter 4. This might have been the intention of those who drafted legislation and policy, or it might provide for the positive uses of discretion described in Chapter 2. This is demonstrated by several of the examples: in Fife, the CSW team was set up using direct government funding related to its initiative 'The Promise', aimed at meeting the needs of looked-after children and their families (which included an important preventative aspect). In Torfaen, the decision to revise services was based on the (at the time) new Wellbeing Act and used its emphasis on co-design. Gary James in Carmarthenshire used an interpretation of the legislation regarding adult safeguarding interventions to ensure that a service met the needs of a neglected group of ARBD sufferers. While in Derry, the multi-disciplinary team (MDT) social workers made full use of the opportunities that the policy roll-out provided to bring community development into practice (and there are many others in Northern Ireland).

What is apparent is that local politicians were not the drivers of CSW approaches; rather, this came from senior managers, as discussed elsewhere in the book. This was true regardless of the political control of the local authorities concerned, whether Conservative Wiltshire, solidly Labour Torfaen, Plaid Cymru in Carmarthenshire or Fife, which has a majority of Scottish National Party (SNP) councillors (though under Labour control through the support of other parties). However, the Fife and Torfaen experiences show that local councillors understand CSW almost instinctively, perhaps because it reduces issues brought to their surgeries, and can therefore be important allies.

Differences

Of the two examples of entire teams devoted to a community model, there are differences. The North Torfaen Wellbeing Team set out to reconfigure their mainstream service to older and vulnerable adults in their locality. The Fife CSW team, on the other hand, were established outside mainstream services (but initially funded and managed through their local authority's children's social work service) to build a preventative community-based service that would not, at least initially, take on statutory referrals. As explained in Chapter 5, the team's work includes complex 'enhanced support' to individuals and families that might well be otherwise dealt with by mainstream statutory teams; this has arisen naturally, particularly since they started taking referrals from general practitioners (GPs). Therefore, while the team do not undertake the formal care management and child assessments of their colleague teams at this stage, it would not require a big jump for them to extend to these tasks for people they are working with already; this carries the potential for gradual change to overall mainstream service delivery. While both the Torfaen and Fife examples are focused on prevention through the active interventions of social workers based on relationship-based practice, there is an emphasis in Fife on community development and co-production, while in Torfaen, this is secondary to the tasks associated with individual well-being. Although the two initiatives set out from different starting places, emerging differences in the way the overall CSW model is put into practice must be expected when, as described in Chapter 3, this is based on co-design and co-production at the base level within communities, which all have different histories, assets and demographics.

The examples also illustrate a variety of funding sources and how local systems and initiatives (A bewildering number in Fife!) have been used creatively to build services. While this has been entirely necessary, it does suggest potential difficulties in sustaining services when short-term rather than core funding (as in Torfaen) is used as a bedrock. Several contributors referred to their practice of offering student placements – refreshing mentions against a background of a general shortage of local authority placements (Narey, 2014; SWEP, 2022). Chapter 10 will look at social work education and its place (or otherwise) in building community social work in more detail.

10

Climate change and community social work

Introduction

There is little dispute as we head into the second quarter of the 21st century that climate change is real and presents a threat to the security of people across the planet. Natural disasters caused by the effects of global warming on weather systems and rising water levels are already causing regular catastrophes in the Global North, which has always considered itself immune from such phenomena. International agreement through the annual Conference of the Parties (COP) to curb carbon dioxide and other greenhouse gases by reducing fossil fuel extraction and use seems to be failing to achieve the progress required and if global warming reaches the levels predicted (a 3°C increase on pre-industrial levels by 2100, being 1.1°C over these already in 2019), areas of the world will be overwhelmed by floods and life-threatening heatwaves (bringing fires and water and food shortages) (IPCC, 2018). There is a growing literature that associates social work with sustainable development (green policies), environmental justice and climate disaster response (see, for example, Dominelli, 2012, 2023; Smith, 2022; Rao et al, 2023; Boddy and Nipperess, 2023). Margaret Ledwith discusses climate change and climate justice extensively in the 2020 edition of *Community Development – A Critical and Radical Approach* (Ledwith, 2020), quoted elsewhere in this book. Social work commentator Ella Booth (2019) will not be alone in her belief that social workers have a responsibility based on the ethical statements of the British Association of Social Workers (BASW) and the International Federation of Social Workers (IFSW) to become climate change activists and involve themselves in protests, such as those organised by Extinction Rebellion. On a similar theme, Whelan (2022: 30) suggests that if social workers are to be 'on the right side of history', they need to show dissent from policies that are failing to tackle climate change effectively. Indeed, a widely read climate change commentator, Andreas Malm (2020: 105), suggests: 'To be radical after all, means aiming at the roots of troubles; to be radical in the chronic emergency is to aim at the ecological roots of perpetual disasters.' While this is in keeping with the radical premise of this book, it takes us no nearer to the actuality of day-to-day social work practice in communities.

As a concept, green social work in response to concerns about climate change is more about influencing policy at the local, national and international levels than related to possibilities through typical interactions with service users. Its components might be applicable to other professions and to good citizenship generally. This is evident in the model suggested by Dominelli (2012: 194):

> It involves social workers working closely with people in their communities and through their everyday life practices to:
>
> • Respect all living things alongside their socio-cultural and physical environments;
> • Develop empowering and sustainable relationships between people and their environments;
> • Advocate for the importance of embedding the social in all economic activities including those aimed at eradicating poverty;
> • Question the relevance of an industrial model of development that relies on over-urbanisation and over-consumption as the basis for social progress; and
> • Promote social and environmental justice.

The IFSW adopted a statement containing a set of principles that reflect such aspirations. The suggested actions – raising awareness, lobbying, mobilising, research and training (that is, through social work education) – lacked reference to addressing the day-to-day issues that bring people to social work (quoted in full in Dominelli, 2023: 104–6).

Reviewing the science on climate change for a social work audience in North America, Professor Robert Hawkins (2023: 232) describes how Canada and the US were ravaged by fires in the summer of 2023 (the hottest on record): 'creating deforestation, loss of life and property ... smoke also creates health issues and ironically, even more carbon emissions to the atmosphere'. He goes on to describe the increasing pattern of storms and floods, the acidification of the oceans, the loss of water supplies, and other very worrying features (Hawkins, 2023). Hawkins, in common with other commentators, remarks that while the Global South will suffer more from all these trends because of more widespread chronic levels of poverty, a lack of robust infrastructure and housing, and geography, the poor in the Global North will also suffer disproportionately (and already are). The people predominantly served by social work services will be unable to afford to ameliorate climate change effects through where and how they live, will have to pay more for scarce food, water and energy sources, and are more likely to encounter consequent ill health.

This chapter will examine how issues arising from climate change are already having an adverse impact on communities and why community social work (CSW) has very practical relevance as a strategy to build resilience and help tackle the harm caused by a changing environment. In 2015, the United Nations (UN) published its 17 Sustainable Development Goals. These include no poverty, zero hunger, good health and well-being, quality education, gender equality, clean water and sanitation, affordable and clean energy, reduced inequalities, sustainable cities and communities, responsible consumption and production, and climate action (United Nations, 2023). These offer useful and useable aspirational goals for community development interventions (Ledwith, 2020) and are applicable to CSW approaches and goals.

A summary of the impact of climate change on poor communities in the UK

There are a number of factors that are making life hard for people in poorer communities that relate to climate change; for example, housing of a poor standard that is not proofed against the effects of the weather will become more of an issue with the onset of extremes of weather. Housing is in crisis anyway, with reductions of social housing builds since the onset of austerity, and house purchase being beyond those on low wages. This forces more people into fewer properties and is especially hard hitting for the young (Dorling, 2023).

Resource scarcity will also impact most upon the poor, whether in terms of rising energy prices bringing fuel poverty, rising food prices as staples like wheat become more problematic to produce on the scale needed to feed the world and the movement of people away from areas of the world that cannot sustain life (and typically beset by wars over control of what resources they do have). Added to all this are health issues caused by weather extremes and the effects of damp, uninsulated housing lacking air conditioning. Our health service is failing, and the wealthy (and not so wealthy) are increasingly turning to private healthcare to avoid lengthy waiting lists (Dorling, 2023).

The summary of factors so far has focused on the effects of gradual change, but recent experience suggests that sudden disasters, such as drought and flooding, will impact on an increasing and largely unforeseeable level. The poor, who are unlikely to have resources to fall back upon, will suffer disproportionally, and there is already evidence that this is exactly what has happened in North America and Australia with their experiences of floods and forest fires (Hawkins, 2023). The poor are also those whose consumption levels contribute least to climate change. Weather changes will impact geographically vulnerable communities: those near woodland and moorland in the case of fire, and those in coastal areas or near rivers and on low-lying flood plains in the case of flooding.

Examples in practice

Social workers are trained to work with individuals, and this book has argued that where groups of people are encountering common issues affecting their family and personal lives, then social work has a role beyond that of traditional casework and case management. Issues relating to climate change will not discriminate, and while some will be more vulnerable to its effects than others (through individual circumstances as well as the ability through wealth to exercise choice), they offer very necessary opportunities for CSW approaches. However, as argued throughout this book, this cannot be based upon well-intentioned interventions by activists to bring urgent matters to the attention of people who might have other immediate concerns. Press reports suggest that Just Stop Oil activists in the UK who have engaged in protests that have impeded people's ability to go about their day-to-day lives have encountered a negative reaction. As these words are written, the UK government's commitment to reducing fossil fuels seems to be wavering in the name of a requirement for economic growth, which, among other objectives, is considered necessary to reduce poverty and increase work opportunities (premises questioned by climate change activists [see Arkbound Foundation, 2021]). Under such circumstances, it should be no surprise that climate change awareness and concern are not a priority to many people struggling with cost-of-living increases and immediate poverty. The consequence is that approaches based on concerns about climate change are unlikely to find resonance within working-class communities, but CSW approaches must focus on issues that are voiced by people in the communities and not imposed upon them, however benignly, by outside agencies. The examples that follow are based on this basic principle.

Example 1: Resilience building

In some parts of the world, social workers in communities are being called upon to respond to problems associated with droughts and earthquakes. In the UK, it is more likely that emergency response will follow flooding, storm damage, wildfires or infrastructure-paralysing snowfalls. Such crisis intervention is of interest to social workers (and community social workers embedded within communities might well be involved) (Dominelli, 2023).

Localised disaster response works best when led and controlled by local people and the agencies they already know and trust in their communities. The author had direct experience of this during a snow emergency in 2013, when attempts to control and respond from outside were not always helpful, bordering on the farcical, because some were designed around bureaucratic requirements rather than local knowledge (Turbett, 2014). Examples included compulsory visits by drafted-in social work staff to people already known to be safe and quite unhelpful media management that ignored the needs of people without electricity supply, whose only means of information was through their battery-powered radios. What did work well was effected by the local social work and health staff, who managed to largely take matters into their own hands with the help of trusted local community activists.

In terms of resilience building, it is contended that fostering proactive solutions from within communities can be a unique social work contribution to disaster planning (Smith, 2022; Hawkins, 2023). Communities that are prone to flooding are an obvious space for such activity, but heavy snowfalls that paralyse communication, infrastructure and power supplies can occur almost anywhere. In the case of obviously vulnerable communities, such as those that are low-lying and flood-prone, the ones with a preponderance of owner-occupied housing are more likely to already have an effective voice articulated to those in power; this is less likely to be the case with marginalised communities and ones where social housing predominates. This was demonstrated with the Grenfell fire in London, a preventable tragedy that resulted in the deaths of 72 people, where the concerns of residents had been consistently ignored (Dominelli, 2023). CSW, with its premise of upstream preventative interventions, is ideal for helping bring resilience to vulnerable communities.

Throughout the UK, the Civil Contingencies Act 2004 (with associated Scottish regulations) governs local emergency planning. The author, who lives on a Scottish island prone to climate-change-related ferry cancellations on an increasing level, has been involved (as a volunteer) in plans for emergency rest centres for people stranded on the island; this has involved emergency planners and various local authority agencies, including social workers, the police and volunteers.

Example 2: Reducing waste

There is a scene in the US TV series *Madmen* (about the New York advertising industry in the 1960s) when the central character Don Draper, a senior executive, takes his family for a picnic in their brand-new and super-huge gas-guzzling car. As they finish, he tosses his drink can away nonchalantly while his wife shakes the detritus from the picnic blanket onto the grass. They then all turn their backs and walk the few steps back to their car without a thought. That short scene, an aside to the main plot, will shock most viewers and demonstrates that we have come some way in recent years with our regard for how we impact the environment: littering is now universally regarded as anti-social and unacceptable. However, we have a long way to go to overcome the throwaway culture encouraged by advertising within a consumerist society.

Food poverty in the UK is estimated to affect 4.7 million people (7 per cent of the population, including 12 per cent of all children) who meet the definition accepted by the UK government (House of Commons Library, 2023). This has become the subject of national campaigns: the Right To Food Campaign, started by Labour Member of Parliament (MP) Ian Byrne in 2021 and supported by a number of trade unions, calls for universal school meals, the factoring in for food by the government when setting minimum wage and benefit levels, the independent enforcement of legislation, community kitchens, and food security as a consideration in all areas of policy making by the government (see: https://www.ianbyrne.org/righttofood). Relating this to social work and the need for food security, social worker Dominic Watters started a campaign in 2021, Food is Care, based on his own experiences of poverty as a single parent on benefits (Community Care, 2022).

It is estimated that the UK produces 9.4 million tons of food waste annually, of which 6.4 million tons are edible – the equivalent of 15 million meals (House of Lords Library, 2021). This is a strange dichotomy when viewed through the prism of widespread food poverty. Various initiatives are under way across the country to reduce this food waste, which contributes to climate change by creating annual greenhouse gas emissions equivalent to 3.5 million cars (Which? Online, 2019). Work to address food waste meets UN sustainable development targets and Westminster government policies to meet climate change targets. Funding is therefore available for specific projects that reduce waste and deploy surplus foodstuffs to food banks and other forms of redistributive activity.

Social workers supporting local communities can help initiate food redistribution projects where they do not exist, and many third sector organisations are already involved across the country. In seeking inspiration for this chapter, the author put out a call on social media to find out more about local food sharing: within hours, a number of social work colleagues provided information on local organisations that they knew of, including in Thurrock and Southend in Essex, Sheffield in South Yorkshire, and Glasgow and East Lothian in Scotland. Clearly, such self-help activity is now commonplace and sits alongside the food banks that are to be found in most communities. Supermarkets are keen to reduce their use of landfill and pass on out-of-date (but safe and edible) foodstuffs through food-share schemes, often through the national FairShare charity, which coordinates this for 8,500 UK front-line community organisations. The Co-Op, which has links with the trade union and labour movement, invites local organisations to contact their local stores directly to arrange evening food collections (see: https://www.coop. co.uk/environment/food-share). Conscious involvement in such developments offers an opportunity to educate and raise the awareness of people about climate change and the causes of food poverty, bringing to life the social pedagogy of Freire discussed in Chapter 2.

Waste that adds to landfill, environmental despoilation and greenhouse gas emissions is not confined to food. Our capitalist system of economics encourages the short-term use and early replacement of household items, furniture and clothing. While past generations revered recycling as part of the natural order, market-based business production based on limitless growth has pushed this aside. The result is the unnecessary production of cheap items, many of which are transported around the world from manufacturing bases in China and other low-wage economies of South-East Asia.

Local recycling schemes are becoming more widespread for furniture and household items, and charity shops recycle clothes within communities (in contrast to recycling banks for clothes that fund-raise but typically export content to the Global South). One well-established not-for-profit organisation in Devon, ReFURNISH, has a number of shops that collect and sell furniture, clothing and small electrical items, as well as books and other bric-a-brac (see: https://www.refurnish.org.uk). Their services include lending out suits and shoes for interviews and funerals, giving out school uniforms, and lending practical support to refugees and asylum seekers – all for free. Any profit from sales is used to cover costs and staffing, including the employment and reskilling of long-term unemployed people. This kind of community enterprise benefits communities by addressing waste and might be replicated elsewhere.

An ambitious waste avoidance enterprise can be found in Fife (and spreading elsewhere): a partnership between the global giant Amazon, which has a warehouse in the area, and the Cottage Family Centre, a local third sector organisation in Kirkcaldy that offers support services to struggling parents of children up to the age of 16 (see: www.thecottagefamilycentre.org.uk). The Cottage Centre is run along community development lines and includes parents in its management and organisation. The partnership with Amazon (known as 'The Big Hoose Project'), an idea of their patron, former UK Prime Minister Gordon Brown, involves the distribution of new goods that have been replaced by new lines, which would otherwise go to landfill. It includes large electrical appliances as well as furniture, and the Amazon project has attracted funds to employ staff and establish a warehouse base. Again, local people in need (based on referral from social services and other official agencies) are being helped, and a contribution is being made to tackling climate-changing waste. Such ideas can be spurred through community development activity facilitated by social workers who understand their communities and are skilled in relationships, networking and motivating people to challenge their limitations and oppression.

Waste is avoided through community food production, and community gardens are spreading as a movement across the country. In Chapter 6, the Clarendon Medical Practice community allotment was described – an initiative that has brought mental well-being to its users and acted as a hub for other activities, being an example of CSW at its best.

Also, in Northern Ireland, the An Tobar project is a community farm in South Armagh whose purpose is to involve the local community in wellness activity and sustainable food production. The project was initiated by two sisters who had the idea of transforming a horticultural centre. The farm is now used by social workers locally who support involvement from those with physical and intellectual disabilities and mental ill health, people with drug issues and in recovery, young people, prisoners, ex-offenders, terminal patients, and older people (Northern Ireland Department of Health, 2023). Feedback suggests improved well-being and a sense of worth and purpose from involvement in animal care, food growing and other farming activities (Northern Ireland Department of Health, 2023).

Example 3: Challenging fuel poverty

Fuel poverty is commonly defined in the UK as spending 10 per cent or more of household income on fuel; on this basis, more than one million households in England and Wales are in 'extreme fuel poverty', as they spend more than 20 per cent of income on energy. This factor pushes people into more general poverty characterised by food and other health-related deficits (for further information, see: https://policy.friendsoftheearth.uk). Energy prices are affected by global politics, international trade agreements and competition, with more regard for profits than the needs of poor consumers. Despite an element of regulation to oversee competition, it is only in exceptional circumstances, such as the pandemic, that the government will step in to provide additional support for home energy costs. Generally, fuel prices are dictated by international markets and are likely to rise as energy needs increase through climate change (while warmer winters will reduce the need for heating, hot summers will increase the need for cooling). Prices are generally likely to increase as food supplies across the world depend on transport, with attendant fuel costs.

One practical means to challenge corporate interests and increase local control is through community energy schemes based on sustainable power generation. In Brixton, South London, a local social enterprise, Brixton Energy, has created three solar energy schemes and launched an energy-efficiency fund that provides local jobs insulating homes and reducing heat loss from homes. One of the directors, Agamemnon Otero, says:

> There's a woman lives here, she's at the bottom of everything. She's got four kids, she's a single mum. She said: 'this is the best thing. I'm saving money on my energy bills, my kids are really into it, they came to the community workshops.' She didn't say 'I want it, I feel really good about myself', she said 'I just hope this can go to other estates.' (Hopkins, 2013: 128–9)

This is another concrete idea that challenges climate change and achieves local ownership and control, as well as a practical way of building community resilience.

Chapter 5, describing the Fife CSW team, gave examples of their use of gathering points in the community where they were able to network with people and offer support with commonly experienced as well as personal issues. The warmth centres that are being established in many communities, where people unable to afford to heat their own homes can meet together in a comfortable and neighbourly setting, offer great opportunities for such CSW interventions, as well as a forum to discuss fuel poverty and other matters.

Example 4: Climate refugees

Those escaping life-threatening economic hardship caused by climate change (drought and famine, floods, and other disasters), whom we shall call 'climate refugees', have no recourse to seek asylum under the 1951 Geneva Convention. This means that they have no rights in any country in which they might seek residence. This seems extraordinary given the scale of environmental catastrophe being experienced in parts of the Global South, but perhaps not so given the rise in the Global North of nationalism and the marking out of borders to resist immigration. Most are therefore displaced internally, bringing massive pressures on fragile economies. The figures are overwhelming, with an estimated number of internal migrants by 2050 of 86 million in sub-Saharan Africa, 49 million in East Asia and the Pacific, 40 million in South Asia, 19 million in North Africa, 17 million in Latin America, and 5 million in Eastern Europe and Central Asia (IOM, 2021). As suggested at the start of this chapter, social workers have a duty to argue that comparatively wealthy nations like the UK should share the burden of climate change migration – especially when it is our consumption levels that are bringing on the crisis rather than the actions of the victims. Africa as a continent is responsible for 4 per cent of global carbon dioxide emissions, but some regions (especially sub-Saharan Africa) are suffering from climate-change-related risks from food and water insecurity, communal conflict over resources and land use, resource conflicts across borders (unsustainable extraction fuelled by external Global North interests), and consequent forced migration and displacement (Noyoo, 2022).

Climate migrants will inevitably find their way to the Global North and overcome the barriers that are in place to prevent and deter such population movement. They should be treated in the same way as those escaping persecution (and with arguable cases under the Geneva Convention) and supported in every way possible. The argument here is that it is not the business of social workers to divide refugees into categories – the deserving and undeserving – but to listen to their stories and support their integration and independence. As there is a strong interrelation between the experiences that cause migration, it should not matter whether the immediate cause is war, persecution, poverty or climate change (Dominelli, 2023). Such work will be inevitably hampered by an asylum and refugee system in the UK that seeks to deter all population movement from the Global South, described by many commentators as racist and inspired by attitudes harking back to colonial times (Webber, 2012; Eddo-Lodge, 2022). Such attitudes permeate down through society and fuel racism and victim blaming at the neighbourhood level. Social workers can play a role in breaking down barriers and challenging racist attitudes through CSW activity.

The refugee and asylum experience is often one of marginalisation and social isolation. Bringing people together can help to overcome trauma. A flexible CSW approach in Manchester with women asylum seekers is described by Berry (2019): the 'Rise and Shine' group involved women from a number of African countries and Bangladesh, all of whom had a strong religious Christian or Muslim faith but were from various backgrounds, some were single and some were married, and some had children in the UK or 'back home'. They were able to share stories, pray for one another, cook meals together and discuss what it means to endure the insecurity and poverty of the UK's asylum system.

Conclusion

Climate change is no longer a contention of some in the scientific community but a fact accepted by governments internationally, even if their response does not always suggest that they see the urgency in addressing the negative impacts now being increasingly experienced across the world. Climate change is manifested in many different ways, though mostly through the manner in which human actions are impacting the environment, much of which is reversible. This chapter has looked at this from a CSW perspective and suggested that this social work model is well placed to be practised in a way that can help disadvantaged communities deal with climate change. While traditional social workers might be deployed to respond in the wake of a disaster, workers already embedded in the community concerned might offer more through their networking and local knowledge. They are also well placed to help build resilience through the preventative and proactive approaches that are essential components of CSW.

11

Community social work within social work education

Jane Pye

Introduction: The context of social work education

Arguably, social work education, in terms of both its classroom teaching and practice placements, is the place where future practitioners' values, understandings and approaches to their practice are formed. Its influence on the whole of the social work profession should therefore not be underestimated. This chapter will briefly explore the origins of social work education, its role in the framing of the social work profession, the relevance of regulation and some of the challenges that social work educators face. This will help explain why it is that community social work (CSW) is not widely taught as a core approach to social work practice in the UK. The chapter will then go on to consider how embedding pedagogical practices that promote CSW is possible in social work education, even within the restrictions of the neoliberal university. Before continuing, a note on language is important. In this chapter, CSW is referred to in line with the philosophy and practice set out in previous chapters of this book. Individualised casework or a case-management approach will be used to define the most common approach to social work in the UK currently (Smith and Whyte, 2008), that is, an approach in which practitioners have a 'caseload' allocated to them and they work on an individual basis with the person or family in need of support rather than the locus of practice being communities.

The history of social work in the UK is well documented (see, for example, Bamford, 2015; Pierson, 2021). Such accounts outline how social work has developed in line with the political and economic ideologies of the times. Social work is not a neutral or objective activity; it is always influenced by and embedded in the 'social' because its very nature is a desire to address the suffering and hardship that citizens experience because of membership of our social world. It is possible to trace the development of social work from its voluntary and philanthropic origins in the late 1800s to the tightly regulated profession that it has become today (Burt, 2022). The development from the wide-ranging, disparate and inconsistent activities that had grown in response to a desire to support those experiencing difficulties to the social work that we know today has largely been brought about by the professionalisation of the activities. This professionalisation included the development of social work education, with both the Universities of Liverpool and Birmingham being forerunners in the early 1900s. The London School of Economics was also and remains influential, and when based there in the 1950s, Eileen Younghusband suggested that social work education should focus on casework as its approach to social work (Burt, 2022), though there is evidence that she also talked about the important role that community development should play as an approach in social work (Heenan, 2004). The early days of social work education, in its attempts to professionalise and form an identity for social work, contributed to the development of the individualised casework model as the dominant approach to practice. This was further cemented by the rise of psychological approaches to supporting people throughout the 1950s–60s, which advocated for a 'client–worker' relationship in which the worker was considered the expert (Howe, 2009).

The political and economic picture in the UK in the 1970s is well acknowledged and touched upon elsewhere in this book. This period is significant in the history of social work, as the greater belief in society as a collective force for good influenced social work's engagement with its community-based roots. This period is when we perhaps see social work at its most radical, reflecting the very serious concerns about inequality, discrimination and oppression prevalent in UK society. Individually experienced social difficulties were firmly linked with their sociological explanations, and this 'macro' approach to social work was reflected in practice. However, social work could not withstand the major shifts in political ideology of the 1980s, which transported the neoliberal project into the social fabric of the UK. The resultant managerialism saw social workers re-identified as 'case managers', thus contributing to the conceptualisation of people who were experiencing some form of personal or social distress or challenge as individual 'cases' rather than members of an unfair and unequal society (Dominelli, 2007). CSW has since been on the periphery of UK social work, as the domination of the individualised casework or case-management model continues. A legitimate question is whether this approach is adequate when thinking about the global challenges we face as a society, especially those challenges related to climate change.

Social work education (And training?)

The conception of what social work is in the UK is contested, and as a result, so is what social work education should focus on (Cleary, 2018). There is research evidence to indicate that the gap between education and practice remains, with students feeling that their education did not prepare them for the realities of practice. This can perhaps be understood as higher education institutions (HEIs) trying to hold on to a 'broad' conception of social work rooted in social justice when practice realities represent a 'narrow' approach to social work that focuses on statutory tasks (Higgins, 2015). A CSW model fits with the broad approach, which is not the dominant approach that we see in practice. These different ways of conceptualising social work were highlighted in 2014 with the publication of two reports on social work education by Croisdale-Appleby (2014) and Narey (2014). It seemed rather odd at the time that two government departments commissioned two separate reports into social work education, with the Department of Health commissioning Croisdale-Appleby and the Department of Education commissioning Narey, who was tasked to focus on children's services. These two reports drew almost opposing conclusions about social work education. Croisdale-Appleby argued for social work education to develop students' understanding of the context of social work and its roots in social issues. For Croisdale-Appleby, social work education must be founded on a clear research and theoretical basis, indicating the importance of critical thinking within the educational experience. For Narey, this approach to social work was not seen as conducive to its primary aim, which is about safeguarding vulnerable children. Narey conceptualised social work as technical practice and made an argument for specialisms in social work. In the (almost) ten years since these reports were published, neither can be seen to have had the impact that was perhaps first expected, but they are excellent examples of how the conceptualisation of what social work is leads naturally to suggestions about what social work education should look like.

Although rather blunt, it is possible to consider these different conceptions as aligned to theoretical questions about the interaction of structure and agency (Giddens, 1984) when understanding the 'causes' of social problems, leading to questions about whether social work should be approached on a micro or macro level – 'micro' refers to practice located at the individual level and 'macro' at a more societal or community level (Knight and Gitterman, 2018). Clearly, these different approaches reflect different understandings of where the origin of social difficulties experienced by individuals and families lie: either in individual failures or in structural and systemic societal failures. The connection here with the individualised casework or case-management approach and the wider focus of CSW is obvious. The domination of the individualised casework approach in social work frames people who use services as the site or locus of intervention; it pathologises people and serves to ensure that they are considered responsible for the social difficulties they are facing, with little acknowledgement of inequality, poverty, disadvantage, oppression and marginalisation. CSW, on the other hand, approaches practice from a sociological perspective and considers how to strengthen and empower communities as a whole as a method of addressing disadvantage and effecting social change. At its best, it can mobilise communities and be experienced as emancipatory.

Again, in a rather simplistic analysis used here to make a point, social work education has largely fallen in line with the individualised approach. Some equate this with a 'training'-orientated approach to becoming a qualified social worker rather than a broader educational approach. A training approach foregrounds tasks and skills. Such an approach can arguably lead to a reductionist competency approach to practice that meets the requirements of employers (Dominelli, 1996). An educational approach is one that provides a broader framing of social issues as connected to power, politics, economics and the oppression and marginalisation of some groups of people in our communities. There are clear connections here with Narey's (2014) and Croisdale-Appleby's (2014) conceptions of social work. Of course, this is a rather simplistic perception of social work education, and the reality is that presenting it in this binary fashion is not entirely helpful. The argument being made here is that there are difficulties with the individualisation of social problems because it does not hold political ideology and its resultant translation into everyday lives accountable for the very real social problems that they create, which are manifested in people's lives. However, it should also be noted that to only focus on a societal or structural approach to social issues fails to acknowledge individuals and their agency and instead presents social problems as something that members of our communities can do almost nothing to change on a day-to-day basis. Agency can translate to social action through collectivity and challenge social problems (McLafferty Bell et al, 2019); therefore, there is a role for social work at both the micro and the macro levels. The issue that we currently have in both social work practice and education is that there is no balance: a sociological approach to practice in the form of real CSW is rare and unacknowledged as a genuine and worthwhile alternative or perhaps complementary approach to the individualisation that dominates. That is not to say that social work education in the UK does not include a sociological framing of social problems within society. The fact that education includes this perspective seems to be one of the core criticisms of social work education according to Narey (2014), who questions whether social work programmes are producing the 'right kind' of social workers. The argument here is that social work students are rarely explicitly introduced to CSW approaches as a method of working holistically with communities to support communities to challenge structural disadvantage. A concern is that should we continue to inch further towards fully embracing a training approach to social work education, opportunities to help students recognise the role of CSW will be reduced or completely lost. This remains a concern in relation to the so-called 'fast-track' routes and social work apprenticeship routes into social work in England (Hanley, 2022). These routes feel more akin to training (see, for example, the Frontline website https://thefrontline.org.uk/become-a-soc ial-worker/frontline-programme/) and, especially in the case of apprenticeships, are heavily influenced by employers, who, for understandable reasons, want social workers to be able to work within the individualised case-management approach because this aligns with how we have organised services in the UK.

Regulation and education in UK social work

The regulatory bodies in the four nations of the UK have a crucial role to play in the framing of what social work education should look like. Universities and HEIs have no choice but to align their programmes with regulatory requirements to ensure they remain validated. Social work has been a graduate-level profession since 2003–04, when the minimum level of qualification in the UK became degree level. This was a significant period in social work education with the abolition of the Central Council for Education and Training in Social Work (CCETSW) in 2001, which had held responsibility for standards in social work education and the validation of social work qualifying programmes from the early 1970s until the early 2000s. Following the closure of CCETSW, the regulation of social work was devolved to the four UK administrations, perhaps to ensure that each nation was tightly standardising the profession in its own context as an ongoing attempt to continue the perception of social work as a highly regulated profession (Worsley, 2023).

Regulation of social work has sat with relevant bodies in Northern Ireland, Wales, Scotland and England for 20 years now. These regulatory bodies are consistent in their requirements for social workers to be registered with them to confirm their suitability to practise and their setting out of general standards of practice that any registered social worker must adhere to. Regulatory bodies also have a significant role in the validation of social work qualifying programmes, which, in combination with their required standards, means that regulatory bodies are powerful in influencing and shaping the content of social work qualifying programmes at both undergraduate and postgraduate levels. What emerges from a review of these educational regulations is evidence that there is an expectation that students are taught to understand the relevance and importance of 'community' and 'communities', though there is very little explicit mention of CSW or similar approaches to practice.

Welsh social work is regulated by Social Care Wales (SCW), which, in line with other regulators, stipulates what is expected of social workers in their 'Practice guidance for social workers' (SCW, 2019) and outlines expectations for social work degree programmes (SCW, 2021a, 2021b). There is no mention of the word 'community' in expectations for degree programmes, though it is recognised that these documents are not intended to outline specific curriculum content. The practice guidance does make four brief references to 'community' but in relation to working with individuals within communities, not in relation to working with communities holistically (SCW, 2019). The National Occupational Standards (NOSs) for social work in Wales give more detail about what social workers are expected to do and consequently what social work education should prepare them for (SCW, 2011). They have numerous mentions of community and even mention of 'community development', with the NOSs indicating that students are expected to have a grasp of what it means to work with communities, not just individuals. This perhaps reflects the view in Wales that participative citizenship is a key aim when considering ways forward in relation to social care (Redcliffe and Ortiz, 2023).

In Northern Ireland, social work is regulated by the Northern Ireland Social Care Council (NISCC), which stipulates expectations for the conduct and behaviour of qualified social workers and students, maintains the social work register, and, in conjunction with the Department of Health, Social Services and Public Safety, specifies the requirements for the degree in social work in Northern Ireland (Northern Ireland Social Care Council and Department of Health, Social Services and Public Safety, 2015). This 2015 document is comprehensive outlining expectations for the providers of social work education, which, unlike in the other areas of the UK, remains at undergraduate level only (Halton and Wilson, 2013). These regulatory requirements again mention the importance of community throughout and are framed in the expectation that social workers understand its relevance. As Heenan (2004) discusses, social work in Northern Ireland perhaps has a different relationship with community development given the experiences known as 'The Troubles'. Although this has not resulted in CSW being central to practice there, it is perhaps unsurprising that it is in Northern Ireland's uniquely structured post-qualifying arrangements that it is possible for social workers to undertake post-qualifying and post-graduate study in community development (O'Brien et al, 2023).

In Scotland, social work is regulated by the Scottish Social Services Council (SSSC) and the standards required for education are the Standards in Social Work Education (SiSWE) (SSSC, 2019). These standards contain numerous mentions of 'community' and the requirement for communities to be of central concern in social work practice. This perhaps reflects ideas that Scotland is generally more advanced in recognising the value of communities than other contexts (McCulloch and Taylor, 2018), which could be a result of the unique roots of Scottish social work (Smith and Whyte, 2008).

In late 2019, Social Work England (SWE) took over the regulation of social work from the generic Health and Care Professions Council (HCPC) in England. Similarly to other locations, as the regulator, SWE maintains the social work register and sets professional standards (SWE, 2019). These standards make minimal reference to the importance of community, and the standards that qualifying programmes have to meet to remain validated (SWE, 2021) make no mention. Since 2012, social work programmes in England have also aligned themselves with the Professional Capabilities Framework (PCF), developed by the Social Work Reform Board and now hosted by the British Association of Social Workers (BASW, 2018). The PCF is a framework that is well embedded and appreciated within both practice and academic settings. This framework mentions the importance of community throughout and is perhaps seen by educators as a more specific set of guidance about what should be included within social work curricula than the regulator's standards. However, concerns remain in the English context about the crowded, if not confused, landscape of social work education, which is becoming overrun with standards, competency measures and capabilities. Added to those mentioned earlier, the chief social workers in England also have a set of knowledge and skills statements (DfE, 2014; DoH, 2015) stating requirements for their respective areas of practice. Many are concerned about the intention of SWE to add to this picture with the development of their own knowledge, skills and behaviour expectations (SWE, 2022).

Details of what is required and expected in each nation in relation to both social work education and practice are therefore slightly different (Parker, 2020). However, from a review of the numerous standards that govern and influence social work education in the UK, there are some encouraging signs. While none of the nations' requirements for social work explicitly state that social workers must have a firm grasp on what CSW is in order to qualify, there are enough references to suggest that community as a concept, as well as the involvement in communities, should be a very important theme within the educational experiences of students. Added to this, the Quality Assurance Agency for Higher Education, in its subject statement for social work, includes numerous references to the importance of understanding community (QAA, 2019). In the context of this book, this therefore leads to a natural question: why does it appear that social work students are not generally taught about CSW as a legitimate approach to social work practice?

Where is CSW in education?

The UK higher education sector is shaped by our neoliberal times (Ball, 2012). HEIs are places of marketisation, performance management, a focus on outcomes and bureaucratic procedures (Jones, 2022). This context results in questions about the purpose and role of higher education because what we perceive higher education to be influences how it is marketed and measured. Undergraduate programmes are subject to rankings, which are used to make judgements about the quality of the programme despite much criticism of this method of judgement (Tight, 2002). Students are also encouraged to formally provide feedback about their experiences through national surveys, which can appear to be an opportunity to genuinely gather student perspectives but a more critical analysis suggests can be used to examine how to keep students happy and therefore attract more students, thus increasing fee income (Bell and Brooks, 2018), rather than genuinely developing pedagogy and improving educational experiences. A theme prevalent in discussions about the value of higher education in recent years has been the so-called 'employability agenda'. This agenda positions higher education as solely a provider of the future workforce (Ashwin, 2020) and can be therefore criticised for its contribution to capitalism. However, despite these criticisms, it remains stuck in its ways, and while it does so, it gives a platform for future employers to influence university programmes.

Evidence indicates that providers of social work education programmes have serious concerns about how neoliberal marketisation impacts directly on social work education (Clearly, 2018) and the autonomy of social work academics teaching social work programmes (Morley et al, 2017). Social work educators appear to remain committed to teaching from a sociological perspective, or at least to including this within social work qualifying programmes, but the reality of practice settings is that practice is approached from an individualist orientation. This is an incredibly important consideration when analysing why we do not give significant space to CSW in social work: qualifying programmes have become aligned with statutory social work and therefore the needs of the main employer of social workers in the UK (Parker, 2020). The neoliberal university has to respond to what the 'market' requires. This framing of students as consumers means that the market of social work education must align with the requirements of employers to remain at least competitive, if not ultimately to remain in existence.

Employers in statutory settings therefore have a powerful role in influencing social work education. This was firmly cemented when, in 2015, social work teaching partnerships in England were launched (King and Cartney, 2023). This project is an example of how social work education providers were encouraged through, what was experienced by many as, a competitive process to form very formal partnerships with local authorities, who were framed as the lead in the partnerships. While not wishing to ignore some of the very positive aspects of such partnerships, one perception of this project is that social work educators are seen to be 'out of touch' with the reality of practice, and through partnership arrangements, local authorities as employers could explicitly shape social work education to meet their needs. Statutory settings are governed by the neoliberal managerialist project, which values performance measures, processes and accountability rather than relational preventative social work practice underpinned by social justice (Rogowski, 2010). It is disappointing that judgements continue to be made about effective social work based on such performative approaches rather than the relationships that social workers form with the people and communities using services. Again, although a rather simplistic analysis, employers may, on the whole, be more in favour of a 'training' approach to social work education, which aligns with the narrow and technical conception of social work (Morley et al, 2019), as discussed earlier. The statutory sector is under serious pressure after years of austerity, rising referrals and increasing need, creating unfavourable working conditions for social workers (Cummins, 2018; UNISON Scotland, 2019; BASW, 2021a; Miller and Barrie, 2022). Resilience has become a key requirement of social workers (Grant and Kinman, 2012) to enable them to survive in such demanding and, at times, unacceptably tough practice contexts. This state of practice means that employers increasingly want 'ready-made social workers' from qualifying programmes so that they can 'hit the ground running' due to demand. Despite the well-intentioned attempts to support newly qualified social workers, they are still expected to practise in very complex settings and be able to cope with the demands of these complexities. The needs of employers therefore significantly influence social work qualifying programmes, and one can imagine the dilemmas that some educators face when wanting to support students to have a broad and critical understanding of social issues founded on principles of social justice while also being aware of the moral imperative to ensure that newly qualified social workers are as ready for the realities of practice as possible. These realities of practice mean that resilience and an ability to meet the narrow requirements of statutory agencies are needed. A CSW approach is redundant in such practice settings. While employers remain powerful and practice settings approach social work in its narrowest form, it is difficult to see how education providers will be able to foreground teaching CSW.

A pedagogy for CSW?

A theme throughout this chapter so far has been the dichotomy between the individualised casework or case-management approach to social work, which is founded on beliefs about social problems being the fault of individuals, and CSW, which, instead, recognises the significance of societal and structural factors and seeks to challenge these through collective action where possible. So far, this chapter has presented a rather bleak picture of social work education from the perspective of CSW. The lack of explicit requirements from regulators for CSW to be taught, the apparent desire in some settings for the 'training' of social workers rather than their education and the context of the neoliberal university have been explored as reasons for this deficit.

Social work education must find a way of rebalancing the focus of these two approaches, if for no other reason than to highlight that there is an alternative approach to individualised casework; social work *is not* individualised casework, but this approach is so dominant that it is easy to believe that it is. This basic understanding is a useful way for us all to remember the deep connection between social work, political beliefs and ideology. A cynical argument could be that one reason why a CSW approach is not centralised in practice is because of its potential to contribute to collaborative social action that could challenge some of the dominant narratives that serve to blame individuals for the social problems they face. Social work education must equip social workers to be critical; this is a core requirement set out by all four regulatory bodies. Being critical includes this understanding of the political nature of social work, and all social work programmes must ensure that students understand this.

If the first stage, then, is around raising basic awareness of CSW within social work qualifying programmes, questions naturally arise around how to 'teach' the application of this approach. Social work education in the UK relies on practice placement opportunities to help students take the abstract and conceptual into the practice context. However, the reality is that most students will not have the opportunity to work within a CSW approach on placement because it is so rare in social work settings, especially statutory settings. Educators must therefore find creative ways to support students to consider and imagine this different way of working in the classroom.

Experiential learning is often used as a theoretical and practical approach to helping students learn from experiences; in social work settings, these are often experiences that are purposefully created in classrooms for learning purposes (Kirkendall and Krishen, 2015). Experiential learning enables students to have an experience, reflect on it, conceptualise it and then consider how they will put the learning into future practice (Kolb, 2015). There is a growing awareness of the potential of working with students as partners in classroom contexts based on students and educators co-producing and co-creating learning opportunities (Dollinger and Lodge, 2020). This is an approach that may feel fairly comfortable to many social work educators, who are likely to hold dear the value base that such an approach is based on. It includes the requirement for social work educators to be comfortable in relinquishing some of their power within a classroom setting in attempts to 'flatten' the classroom (Congdon and Congdon, 2011). It frames students as experts of their own learning experiences and aims to empower them to consider how they can contribute to the learning process, and it promotes student collective agency. At its best, co-creation is inclusive and values all voices. Its founding principles are drawn from critical pedagogy and a desire to democratise classroom settings (Bovil, 2013). Co-creation as a pedagogical approach to learning can therefore provide students with an experience that is collaborative, inclusive and collective, thus modelling CSW as an approach to working with communities of people.

Future challenges and CSW education

This chapter has argued that the lack of focus and attention in social work education given to CSW is due to the dominance of the individualised casework approach. However, there are glimmers of inspiring and innovative practice, such as those described earlier in this book that harness a CSW approach. Added to these, qualified social workers in Northern Ireland can undertake postgraduate study in community development. In terms of the UK, these are relatively small-scale examples, but they do indicate that a commitment to CSW does remain in some areas of the social work profession. However, while some of us may feel that a CSW approach is more aligned with the social justice value base that should underpin social work, realism is required. In our neoliberal times, we are not going to see a wholesale move to CSW in the UK anytime soon, though elsewhere in this book, CSW is offered as a means to save social work from becoming irrelevant, unrewarding and failing in its central tasks. What we can do is work to ensure that social work as a profession does not forget about CSW, and this can start by ensuring that it is covered in social work education. Indeed, it is educators' responsibility to theoretically and practically explore how to develop and improve social work and how to be ready and equipped for the social problems of contemporary society. There can be no bigger challenge to be faced than that of climate change and the associated environmental injustice. This is a problem on a scale that we have never experienced before, and no individualised approach will tackle it. Social work education must embed an understanding of the potential of CSW as the future of social work in students so that they can be ready for social work to play its part in climate change and its impacts. It would be a progressive regulator that included an explicit obligation for social work education to include CSW approaches within their requirements with climate change in mind.

12

Conclusion: The future of community orientation and community social work

Introduction

This final chapter of the book summarises the substantive content and offers basic guides to the separate but connected thrusts of community orientation and community social work (CSW). The book has argued throughout that CSW offers an attractive preventative and relationship-based model of social work practice that can and should be adapted to local (bottom-up) co-design and co-production.

The examples given, while rare, indicate that this is not just an ideal but, when tested in practice, can have good outcomes. As explained early in the book, they have all been chosen from local authority (and equivalent in Northern Ireland) settings to demonstrate their significance to mainstream service delivery; while there is nothing wrong with CSW being applied in the third sector, particularly by grass-roots community-based organisations, this does not have to be their natural home. It is almost inevitable that this is where they might be found when competing for direct funding is an increasingly found method by which governments try to meet their welfare targets (rather than through core funding to the local authorities providing statutory services [Turbett, 2023a]). The book also criticises the notion that such preventative services should be provided through the currently popular medium of community link workers (community connectors) and volunteers. Such services are rarely confined to signposting but are advertised as providing generic low-level direct interventions by staff without social work qualifications and volunteers. It is argued here that properly funded CSW using the skills of qualified social workers can target the same goals, as well as additional ones requiring more expertise, more effectively because the skills required are ones taught in social work training.

Testament is offered through the examples of what is described in the book as 'creativity and artistry'. Although university social work courses in the UK are focused on training for the job, as discussed by Jane Pye in Chapter 11, the efforts of teaching staff to encourage creative and critical thinking must be working for some students, despite Jane Fenton's fears discussed at the start of Chapter 2.

Finally, comment must be made about the sustainability of CSW initiatives: real thought has to be given to this when seeking change that emanates from pilot projects. Changes in management and insecure funding arrangements (as true for local authorities now as it has always been for the third sector) can jeopardise new projects and nullify hard work and hope. This book has offered examples of initiatives that were under way at the time it was written (in all likelihood, one will have been erased by the time the book is published). The author knows of others that have come and gone in recent years, along with all the examples from the 1980s. Their passing does not diminish their value, and they shine from the past as beacons of hope for those of us who want to see social work return to the promise of its roots. Government policies that favour CSW as a mainstream approach to social work, for the reasons outlined throughout this book, would certainly help, and this seems achievable given repeated commitments to prevention and co-design.

The tables

Community orientation can be practised by anyone if the conditions are right, but CSW requires more in terms of planning and teamwork; those embarking on the CSW journey described in

Table 12.2 might benefit from familiarity with the styles described in Table 12.1. These are presented as general guides and not templates, though it is of course up to the reader to determine how useful and useable they might be.

Last words: a personal note

Writing this book has involved discussions across the UK with people involved in the world of social work, including some with lived experience of being in receipt of services. Among social workers and their managers, responses to the idea of CSW were varied: those brought up in an era of care management and centralised and procedural working methods found it threatening and difficult to conceptualise. The most welcoming were those who undertook professional training before 2000, who believed that the model contains an element missing in most of the practice they had found in their statutory settings. However, they did not necessarily think that it was realisable in today's pressured and cash-strapped environment. There were also younger students and qualified workers who were excited by the idea because they saw it as representing the values and methods that had attracted them towards social work as a career in the first place. Among academics and social work teachers, I have found overwhelming support for CSW, especially among those who support the ideas of critical and radical practice discussed variously by Webb (2023), and I hope they will find substance and hope in Jane Pye's guest chapter. When I have addressed conferences and shared workshop opportunities (some with Jane, and some with colleagues from Fife), I have been happily satisfied with those who have turned out to listen and shown interest in taking the idea back with them; they are the ones who realise the reality, as argued in this book, that the profession has to turn away from the models commonly found in practice if it is to survive as a worthwhile and effective profession that lives up to the core value of promoting social justice. It is not a case of whether CSW can be afforded; rather, it is more that we cannot afford *not* to make such changes.

The book has provided material for those who do want to challenge the status quo and take social work forward to communities, where it can help create a more equal and fair

Table 12.1: Becoming a community-orientated social worker

Task heading	Aim	Method	Book chapter(s) and further Resources	Practice examples from Chapters 5–8
1. Finding the right setting	To judge whether a setting offers a culture suitable for the promotion of community-orientated and generalist practice	Find answers to the following questions: • Is there regular supervision and workload management? • Are supervisors willing to allow deviation from mainstream statutory tasks? • Does the team have the physical (office) space for daily peer support and teamwork (remote/homeworking and hot-desking are not considered conducive to this method)? • Is the office location/team base accessible to the community it serves?	Chapter 2 of this book Hardcastle et al (2011) Mullaly (2010) Turbett (2013)	Carmarthenshire, Wales Torfaen, Wales
2. Understanding poverty and inequality and their impact on communities and individuals	To gain knowledge of issues generally so that this is brought into social work approaches to problem solving, and de-individualising and seeing them in their full context	Reading and taking an interest in current affairs and politics at local and national levels, engaging in campaigning activity, trade union membership and involvement, and professional association membership and involvement	Chapter 2 of this book Wilkinson and Pickett (2010) Mullaly (2010) UNISON UNITE GMB BASW Social Workers Union Social Workers Without Borders	Wiltshire, England Fife, Scotland Derry, Northern Ireland
3. Build support in the workplace for alternative approaches	To encourage and promote support within and beyond the workplace for community orientation and a social justice approach to work	Building support for challenges to popular myths within the workplace that perpetuate oppression – changing the workplace culture Building personal credibility through examples of good practice and positive approaches to tasks	Chapter 2 of this book Baines (2007) Mullaly (2010) Turbett (2013)	Carmarthenshire, Wales Wiltshire, England Derry, Northern Ireland

Table 12.1: Becoming a community-orientated social worker (continued)

Task heading	Aim	Method	Book chapter(s) and further Resources	Practice examples from Chapters 5–8
		Using opportunities to build team identity through methods as diverse as social activities, team-meeting-based discussion and tearoom discussion Through warmth, humour and empathy rather than political correctness and put-downs!	Turbett (2014) Turbett (2023b)	
4. Build community assets	To build and enhance networks in the community, whether with other agencies or community activists, which enable working together for community well-being and individual growth	A start might be made through building up a community profile, which could be a very ambitious project or a simpler personal accumulation of local knowledge Discover what networks already exist, and make a point of building relationships with other agencies' staff, for example, police officers, teachers, third sector staff, community health staff, general practitioners (GPs) and others Find out what community associations exist and consider introductions	Chapters 2 and 3 of this book Hawtin and Percy-Smith (2007)	Carmarthenshire, Wales Torfaen, Wales Fife, Scotland Derry, Northern Ireland Wiltshire, England
5. Creating imaginative solutions to commonly experienced issues	To discover new ways of working with people that empower them to seek their own solutions and act on them, using the artistry and creativity of social workers	Talking to service users collectively as well as individually might throw up suggestions, for example, groupwork programmes, community gardens, workshops, arts and cultural activities, and walking groups	Chapters 2 and 3 of this book	Carmarthenshire, Wales Torfaen, Wales Derry, Northern Ireland Fife, Scotland Wiltshire, England

Table 12.2: Creating a CSW team

Task heading	Aim	Method	Book chapter(s) and further resources	Practice examples from Chapters 5–8
1. Winning hearts and minds	Preparing the ground in the agency for the turn to CSW	Workshops and team presentations with outside speakers Dissemination of basic reading material Identification of champions at all organisational levels	Chapters 2 and 3 of this book	Fife, Scotland Torfaen, Wales Derry, Northern Ireland
2. Identify locality/ community as a potential subject for CSW service	Creation of new social work service, either through the transformation of existing one or through the creation of a parallel CSW team	Comparison of community profiling information, identification of resources required and winning of political support at the local level Open discussions with identifiable community 'leaders' Questions to consider: • Possible locations for CSW, for example, school, GP practice or other community setting? • Will social workers have any statutory responsibilities?	Chapter 3 of this book	Fife, Scotland Torfaen, Wales Derry, Northern Ireland
3. Appointment of responsible manager	Facilitation of development of the CSW model in the locality/community selected	Leadership task: recruitment or secondment of a suitably motivated individual with the ability to motivate others in a new setting	Chapter 3 of this book	Fife, Scotland Torfaen, Wales
4. Recruitment of staff	To create a team whose experiences reflect various aspects of social work, some lived experience and some diversity in background Recruits should embody the knowledge bases in Table 12.1	The interview process might involve community members and, if recruiting further at a later stage, previous or existing users of the CSW service	Chapter 3 of this book	Fife, Scotland

Table 12.2: Creating a CSW team (continued)

Task heading	Aim	Method	Book chapter(s) and further resources	Practice examples from Chapters 5-8
	They should hold in common a wish to explore new areas of social work activity and be able to demonstrate creativity and artistry Larger agencies will need to draw up job descriptions reflecting expected CSW duties, for example, community development as well as assessment skills			
5. Induction	Prepare the team for tasks ahead	Reading material on CSW, and input on basic community development strategies and groupwork theory and practice Introduction to social pedagogy, and consideration of the use of language, meaning of professionalism and working with relationships	Chapter 3 of this book Ledwith (2020) Mullender and Ward (1991) Freire (1994) Russell and McKnight (2022) Mullaly (2010)	Fife, Scotland Torfaen, Wales
6. Community profiling and initial networking	To learn about the community and its assets and issues	Engagement by team members with other front-line staff and activists in existing statutory and third sector agencies Factual information gathering and sharing	Chapter 3 of this book Hawtin and Percy-Smith (2007)	Fife, Scotland Torfaen, Wales Derry, Northern Ireland
7. Going out with the 'blank sheet of paper'	Learning from local community members about their hopes, fears, issues and suggested solutions	Meeting in previously chosen community settings and meeting places Being brave and confident but sensitive about approaching people and groups	Chapter 3 of this book	Fife, Scotland Torfaen, Wales

(continued)

Table 12.2: Creating a CSW team (continued)

Task heading	Aim	Method	Book chapter(s) and further resources	Practice examples from Chapters 5–8
8. Co-production and community engagement	The creation of services that communities feel ownership over	Community engagement exercises, and co-production methods on an ongoing systematic rather than one-off 'community consultation' basis	Chapters 2 and 3 of this book Russell and McKnight (2022)	Fife, Scotland Torfaen, Wales Derry, Northern Ireland
9. Assuming responsibility for statutory duties	To use CSW to cover mainstream areas of work	Method requires negotiation and consideration on a basis peculiar to the team's purpose and context; for example, is the service offered to a particular service group or generic across the range of ages and need? A gradual introduction might be appropriate	Chapters 3 and 9 of this book	Fife, Scotland Torfaen, Wales
10. Reflection-in-action	Learning by trial and error what works and what does not on a day-by-day basis	Individual reflection-in-action and use of collegial and team support	Chapters 3 and 9 of this book Schön (1991)	Fife, Scotland Torfaen, Wales
11. Reflection-on-action	To provide meaningful evaluation of work done (including on a day-to-day basis) that will guide development and aid outside scrutiny from others in the agency and politicians	Systematic and planned opportunity for team evaluation, which can be developed to involve other partners, including service users If resources are available, this could be developed into action research that might help others in the future	Chapters 3 and 9 of this book Schön (1991) Bradbury (2015)	Fife, Scotland Torfaen, Wales
12. Celebration and spreading the word	To use experience gained to broaden the appeal and practice of CSW	Conference opportunities, exhibitions, training presentations, publications, blogs and alternative expressive forms Representations (with community representatives) to politicians and policy makers	Chapter 3 of this book	Fife, Scotland Derry, Northern Ireland Carmarthenshire, Wales Torfaen, Wales Wiltshire, England

society and build the resilience that will be needed as we try to address climate change. It has given coverage to and comment on the historical development and practice of CSW, and it has offered some contemporary examples that have their roots in that history. In true back-to-the-future fashion, it is over to the reader to turn this into some new realities.

References

Allen, D. and GRTSWA (Gypsy, Roma and Traveller Social Work Association) (2022) 'Good practice guidance: understanding the impact of the Police, Crime, Sentencing and Courts Act', https://www.basw.co.uk/resources/good-practice-guidance-understanding-welfare-impact-police-crime-sentencing-courts-act (accessed August 2023).

Allen, D. and Hamnett, V. (2022) 'Gypsy Roma and Traveller children in child welfare services in England', *British Journal of Social Work* 52: 3904–22.

Allen, D. and Hulmes, A. (2021) 'Aversive racism and child protection practice with Gypsy, Roma and Traveller children and families', *Seen and Heard* 31(2): 40–55.

Allen, D. and Riding, S. (2018) 'The fragility of professional competence: a preliminary account of child protection practice with Romani and Traveller children', European Roma Rights Centre, http://www.errc.org/reports--submissions/the-fragility-of-professional-competence-a-preliminary-account-of-child-protection-practice-with-romani-and-traveller-children-in-england (accessed August 2023).

Allum, M. (2020) 'Wiltshire Gypsy, Roma, Traveller and Boater strategy 2020–2025', https://cms.wiltshire.gov.uk/documents/s181346/Appendix%201%20Wiltshire%20Gypsy%20Roma%20Traveller%20and%20Boater%20Strategy%202020-2025.pdf (accessed August 2023).

Arkbound Foundation (ed) (2021) *Climate Adaptation – Accounts of Resilience, Self-Sufficiency and Systems Change*, Glasgow: Arkbound.

Ashwin, P. (2020) *Transforming University Education: A Manifesto*, London: Bloomsbury.

Bailey, R. and Brake, M. (eds) (1975) *Radical Social Work*, London: Edward Arnold.

Baines, D. (2007) *Doing Anti-oppressive Practice: Building Transformative Politicized Social Work*, Nova Scotia: Fernwood.

Ball, S. (2012) 'Performativity, commodification and commitment: an I-Spy guide to the neoliberal university', *British Journal of Educational Studies* 60(1): 17–28.

Bamford, T. (2015) *A Contemporary History of Social Work: Learning from the Past*, Bristol: Policy Press.

Banks, S. (2011) 'Re-gilding the ghetto – community work and community development in 21st century Britain', in Lavalette, M. (ed) *Radical Social Work Today – Social Work at the Crossroads*, Bristol: Policy Press, 165–85.

Banks, S., Butcher, H., Orton, A. and Robertson, J. (2003) *Managing Community Practice – Principles, Policies and Programmes*, 2nd edn, Bristol: Policy Press.

Barclay, P. (1982) *Social Workers – Their Role and Tasks*, London: National Institute of Social Work.

BASW (British Association of Social Workers) (2018) 'Professional capabilities framework', https://www.basw.co.uk/social-work-training/professional-capabilities-framework-pcf (accessed August 2023).

BASW (2021a) *The BASW Annual Survey of Social Workers and Social Work: 2021 Summary Report*, Birmingham: BASW.

BASW (2021b) *BASW England Scoping Review for Children and Family Social Work*, Birmingham: BASW England, https://www.basw.co.uk/system/files/resources/basw_annual_survey_summary_report_2021.pdf (accessed May 2023)

BASW (2022) 'BASW UK statement on anti-Gypsyism and Gypsy, Roma and Traveller rights', https://www.basw.co.uk/basw-uk-statement-anti-gypsyism-and-gypsy-roma-and-traveller-rights (accessed August 2023).

Bell, A.R. and Brooks, C. (2018) 'What makes students satisfied? A discussion and analysis of the UK's national student survey', *Journal of Further and Higher Education* 42(8): 1118–42.

Bennett, R. (1945) *The More We Are Together – Community Centres*, London: Army Bureau of Current Affairs.

Beresford, P. and Croft, S. (1984) 'Welfare pluralism: the new face of Fabianism', *Critical Social Policy* 3(9): 19–39.

Berry, H. (2019) 'Lessons from community work: practices of alliance with asylum seeking women', in Wroe, L., Larkin, R. and Maglajilic, R. (eds) *Social Work with Refugees, Asylum Seekers and Migrants*, London: Jessica Kingsley, 189–204.

Beveridge, W. (1943) *The Pillars of Security*, London: George Allen & Unwin.

Boddy, J. and Nipperess, S. (2023) 'Green social work and social justice', in Webb, S. (ed) *The Routledge Handbook of International Critical Social Work – New Perspectives and Agendas*, London: Routledge, 660–70.

Bonell, C., McKee, M., Fletcher, A. (2016) 'Troubled families, troubled policy making', *British Medical Journal* 355: i5879.

Booth, E. (2019) 'Extinction Rebellion: social work, climate change and solidarity', *Critical and Radical Social Work* 7(2): 257–61.

Bovil, C. (2013) 'Students and staff co-creating curricula – a new trend or an old idea we never got around to implementing?', in Rust, C. (ed) *Improving Student Learning through Research and Scholarship: 20 Years of ISL*, Oxford: The Oxford Centre for Staff and Educational Development, 96–108.

Bradbury, H. (2015) *The Sage Book of Action Research*, London: Sage.

Brady, D. (2009) *Rich Democracies, Poor People: How Politics Explain Poverty*, New York, NY: Oxford University Press.

Brewer, C. and Lait, J. (1980) *Can Social Work Survive*, London: Temple Smith.

Brodie, I., Nottingham, C., Plunkett, I. (2008) 'A tale of two reports: *Social Work in Scotland from Social Work and the Community* (1966) to *Changing Lives* (2006)', *British Journal of Social Work* 38: 697–715.

Burt, M. (2022) 'Introducing social workers: their roles and training', *British Journal of Social Work* 52: 2166–82.

CDP Inter-Project Editorial Team (Community Development Projects Inter-Project Editorial Team) (1977) *Gilding the Ghetto – The State and Poverty Experiments*, London: CDP Inter-Project Editorial Team.

Cemlyn, S., Greenshields, M., Burnett, S., Mathews, Z. and Whitwell, C. (2009) 'Inequalities experienced by Gypsy and Traveller communities: a review', Equality and Human Rights Commission, Research Report No. 12, https://www.equality humanrights.com/sites/default/files/research-report-12-inequ alities-experienced-by-gypsy-and-traveller-communities.pdf (accessed August 2023).

Changing Futures Northumbria (2023) 'Our Three Levels of Change', https://www.chamgingfuturesnorthumbria.co.uk/about-us (accessed November 2023).

Cheers, B. (1998) *Welfare Bushed: Social Care in Rural Australia*, Aldershot: Ashgate.

Cheung, J. (2017) 'Practice wisdom in social work: an uncommon sense in the intersubjective encounter', *European Journal of Social Work* 20(5): 616–29.

Clearly, T. (2018) 'Social work education and the marketisation of UK universities', *British Journal of Social Work* 48: 2253–71.

Collier, K. (2006) *Social Work with Rural Peoples*, 3rd edn, Vancouver: New Star.

Community Care (2022) ' "It's taking a deprived single dad to highlight issues of food insecurity": a newly qualified social worker is using his experiences of poverty to campaign for change and inform other practitioners', 24 March, https://www.communitycare.co.uk/2022/03/24/its-taking-a-depri ved-single-dad-to-highlight-issues-of-food-insecurity/ (accessed January 2024).

Congdon, G. and Congdon, S. (2011) 'Engaging students in a simulated collaborative action research project: an evaluation of a participatory approach to learning', *Journal of Further and Higher Education* 35(2): 221–31.

Corrigan, P. and Leonard, P. (1978) *Social Work Practice under Capitalism: A Marxist Approach*, London: Macmillan.

Cottam, H. (2018) *Radical Help – How We Can Remake the Relationships between Us and Revolutionise the Welfare State*, London: Virago.

Craig, G., Mayo, M., Popple, K., Shaw, M. and Taylor, M. (eds) (2011) *The Community Development Reader – History, Themes and Issues*, Bristol: Policy Press.

Cree, V. (1995) *From Public Streets to Private Lives – The Changing Task of Social Work*, Aldershot: Avebury.

Croisdale-Appleby, D. (2014) 'Re-visioning social work education an independent review', https://assets.publishing.service.gov.uk/government/uploads/system/uploads/attachment_data/file/285788/DCA_Accessible.pdf (accessed August 2023).

Crossley, S. and Lambert, M. (2017) '"Looking for trouble?" Critically examining the UK government's Troubled Families programme', *Social Policy and Society* 16(1): 81–5.

Crouch, D. (2011) *The Strange Non-death of Neoliberalism*, Cambridge: Polity Press.

Cummins, I. (2018) *Poverty, Inequality and Social Work*, Bristol: Policy Press.

Dawson, C. (2020) 'Perceptions of social work summary report: research amongst the general public and those with lived experience of social work', Social Work England, https://www.socialworkengland.org.uk/media/3323/crd-public-perceptions-report-summary.pdf (accessed August 2023).

DfE (Department for Education) (2014) 'Knowledge and skills for child and family social work', https://assets.publishing.service.gov.uk/government/uploads/system/uploads/attachment_data/file/338718/140730_Knowledge_and_skills_statement_final_version_AS_RH_Checked.pdf (accessed August 2023).

DH (Department of Health) (2015) 'Knowledge and skills statement for social work in adult services', https://assets.publishing.service.gov.uk/government/uploads/system/uploads/attachment_data/file/411957/KSS.pdf (accessed August 2023).

Dollinger, M. and Lodge, J. (2020) 'Staff–student co-creations in higher education: an evidence-informed model to support futures design and implementation', *Journal of Higher Education Policy and Management* 42(5): 532–46.

Dominelli, L. (1996) 'Professionalizing social work: anti-oppressive practice, competencies and postmodernism', *British Journal of Social Work* 26: 153–75.

Dominelli, L. (2007) 'Contemporary challenges to social work education in the United Kingdom', *Australian Social Work* 60(1): 29–45.

Dominelli, L. (2012) *Green Social Work: From Environmental Crisis to Environmental Justice*, Cambridge: Polity Press.

Dominelli, L. (2023) *Social Work Practice during Times of Disaster – A Transformative Green Social Work Model for Theory, Education and Practice in Disaster Interventions*, London: Routledge.

Dorling, D. (2018) *Peak Inequality – Britain's Ticking Time Bomb*, Bristol: Policy Press.

Dorling, D. (2023) *Shattered Nation – Inequality and the Geography of a Failing State*, London: Verso.

Downs, F. (1945) *Theirs is the Future – Youth Services*, London: Army Bureau of Current Affairs.

Dustin, D. (2007) *The McDonaldization of Social Work*, Abingdon: Routledge.

Eddo-Lodge, R. (2022) *Why I'm No Longer Talking to White People about Race*, 2nd edn, London: Bloomsbury.

Edwards, D. and Parkinson, K. (2018) *Family Group Conferences in Social Work – Involving Families in Social Care Decision Making*, Bristol: Policy Press.

England, H. (1986) *Social Work as Art*, London: Allen & Unwin.

Esping-Anderson, G. (1990) *The Three Worlds of Welfare Capitalism*, Oxford: Polity Press.

Evans, T. and Harris, J. (2004) 'Street level bureaucracy, social work and the (exaggerated) death of discretion', *British Journal of Social Work* 34(6): 871–95.

Fanon, F. (1965 [1961]) *The Wretched of the Earth*, London: MacGibbon & Kee.

Fanon, F. (1986 [1952]) *Black Skin, White Masks*, London: Pluto Press.

Fenton, J. (2019) *Social Work for Lazy Radicals: Relationship Building, Critical Thinking and Courage in Practice,* London: Red Globe.

Ferguson, I. and Woodward, R. (2009) *Radical Social Work in Practice – Making a Difference*, Bristol: Policy Press.

Forde, C. and Lynch, D. (2015) *Social Work and Community Development*, London: Palgrave.

Freire, P. (1996) *Pedagogy of the Oppressed*, London: Penguin.

Freire, P. (1994) *Pedagogy of Hope – Reliving Pedagogy of the Oppressed*, New York: Continuum.

Friends, Families and Travellers (2020) 'Written evidence submitted by Friends, Families and Travellers', CVB0048, https://committees.parliament.uk/writtenevidence/8641/pdf/

Gardner, A. (2014) *Personalisation in Social Work*, 2nd edn, London: Learning Matters.

Garrett, P.M. (2021) 'Against stultifying classifications, for a "new humanism": Franz Fanon's contribution to social work's commitment to liberation', *British Journal of Social Work* 51(8): 2910–27.

Giddens, A. (1984) *The Constitution of Society*, Cambridge: Polity Press.

Ginsberg, A. (ed) (1998) *Social Work in Rural Communities*, 3rd edn, Alexandra, PA: CSWE.

Gramsci, A. (1982) *Selections from the Prison Notebooks*, London: Lawrence & Wishart.

Grant, L. and Kinman, G. (2012) 'Enhancing wellbeing in social work students: building resilience in the next generation', *Social Work Education* 31(5): 605–21.

Greenfields, M. and Rogers, C. (2020) 'Hate: "as regular as rain" – a pilot research project into the psychological effects of hate crime on Gypsy, Traveller and Roma (GTR) communities', https://gateherts.org.uk/wp-content/uploads/2020/12/Rain-Report-201211.pdf (accessed August 2023).

Griffiths Report (1988) *Community Care: An Agenda for Action*, London: HMSO.

Hadley, R. and McGrath, M. (1984) *When Social Services Are Local – The Normanton Experience*, NISW Library No. 84, London: George, Allen & Unwin.

Hadley, R., Cooper, M., Dale, P. and Stacey, G. (1987) *A Community Social Worker's Handbook*, London: Tavistock Publications.

Halton, C. and Wilson, G. (2013) 'Changes in social work education in Ireland', *Social Work Education*, 32(8): 969–71.

Hanley, J. (2022) 'Better together: comprehensive social work education in England', *Critical and Radical Social Work* 10(1): 127–43.

Hardcastle, D., Powers, P. and Wenocur, S. (2011) *Community Practice – Theories and Skills for Social Workers*, 3rd edn, Oxford: OUP.

Harris, J. (2003) *The Social Work Business*, Abingdon: Routledge.

Harris, J. (2008) 'State social work: constructing the present from moments in the past', *British Journal of Social Work* 38: 662–79.

Harris, J. and White, V. (2018) *The Oxford Dictionary of Social Work and Social Care*, 2nd edn, Oxford: OUP.

Hawkins, R. (2023) 'Social work response to climate change: if we are not already too late', *Social Work Research* 47(4): 231–5.

Hawtin, M. and Percy-Smith, J. (2007) *Community Profiling – A Practical Guide*, 2nd edn, Maidenhead: Open University Press.

Heenan, D. (2004) 'Learning lessons from the past or re-visiting old mistakes: social work and community development in Northern Ireland', *British Journal of Social Work* 34(6): 793–809.

Heenan, D. and Birrell, D. (2011) *Social Work in Northern Ireland – Conflict and Change*, Bristol: Policy Press.

Higgins, M. (2015) 'The struggle for the soul of social work in England', *Social Work Education* 34(1): 4–16.

Hollis, F. (1964) *Casework – A Psycho-Social Therapy*, New York, NY: Random House.

Hopkins, R. (2013) *The Power of Just Doing Stuff: How Local Action Can Change the World*, Cambridge: Green Books.

House of Commons Library (2023) 'Food poverty: households, foodbanks and free school meals', https://commonslibrary.parliament.uk/research-briefings/cbp-9209/ (accessed January 2024).

House of Lords Library (2021) 'In focus – food waste in the UK', https://lordslibrary.parliament.uk/food-waste-in-the-uk/ (accessed January 2024).

Howe, D. (2009) *A Brief Introduction to Social Work Theory*, Basingstoke: Palgrave Macmillan.

Hughes, M. and Wearing, M. (2007) *Organisations and Management in Social Work*, London: Sage.

Hulmes, A. and Unwin, P. (forthcoming) 'Rural social work with Romani and Travellers', in Pye, J. and Turbett, C. (eds) *Rural Social Work in the UK – Themes and Challenges for the Future*, London: Palgrave.

Ideas Fund (nd) About us, https://theideasfund.org/about/about-us (accessed August 2023).

Intergovernmental Panel on Climate Change (eds) (2018) 'Global warming of 1.5°C: an IPCC special report on the impacts of global warming of 1.5°C above pre-industrial levels and related global greenhouse gas emission pathways, in the context of strengthening the global response to the threat of climate change, sustainable development, and efforts to eradicate poverty', www.ipcc.ch/sr15 (accessed January 2024).

IOM (International Organisation for Migration) (2021) 'Human Mobility at COP27', https://environmentalmigration.iom.int/human-mobility-cop27 (accessed January 2024).

James, E., Mitchell, R. and Morgan, H. (2020) *Social Work, Cats and Rocket Science: Stories of Making a Difference in Social Work with Adults*, London: Jessica Kingsley.

Jones, R. (2014) 'The best of times, the worst of times: social work and its moment', *British Journal of Social Work* 44: 485–502.

Jones, R. (2023) 'The Northern Ireland review of children's social care services report', https://www.cscsreviewni.net/publications/report-independent-review-childrens-social-care-services-northern-ireland (accessed July 2023).

Jones, S. (2022) *Universities under Fire*, Switzerland: Palgrave Macmillan.

Kelly, D. and Kennedy, J. (2017) 'Power to people: proposals to reboot adult care and support in Northern Ireland', https://www.health-ni.gov.uk/sites/default/files/publications/health/power-to-people-full-report.PDF (accessed July 2023).

Kidd, C., with Jo, Keith and Marie (2023) 'Working with marginalised adults – learning from experts by experience', in Lee, S. and Oliver, L. (eds) *Social Work Practice with Adults – Learning from Lived Experience*, London: Sage, 85–93.

King, E. and Cartney, P. (2023) 'Teaching partnerships in neoliberal times: promoting collaboration or competition', *Practice: Social Work in Action* 35(1): 5–16.

Kirkendall, A. and Krishen, A.S. (2015) 'Encouraging creativity in the social work classroom: insights from a qualitative exploration', *Social Work Education* 34(3): 341–54.

Knight, C. and Gitterman, A. (2018) 'Merging micro and macro intervention: social work practice with groups in the community', *Journal of Social Work Education* 54(1): 3–17.

Kolb, D.A. (2015) *Experiential Learning: Experience as the Source of Learning and Development*, 2nd edn, London: Pearson Education Inc.

Labour Party (2023a) 'Safe and secure communities', https://www.policyforum.labour.org.uk/commissions/empowered-communities (accessed July 2023).

Labour Party (2023b) 'Public Services that work from the start', https://www.policyforum.labour.org.uk/commissions/public-services-that-work-from-the-start (accessed March 2024).

Langan, M. (2011) 'Rediscovering radicalism and humanity in social work', in Lavalette, M. (ed) *Radical Social Work Today: Social Work at the Crossroads,* Bristol: Policy Press, 153–63.

Ledwith, M. (2020) *Community Development – A Critical and Radical Approach*, 3rd edn, Bristol: Policy Press.

Leeds Council (nd) 'Strengths based social care in Leeds City Council', https://www.ndti.org.uk/assets/files/Strengths-based_social_care_in_Leeds_City_Council_low_res.pdf (accessed November 2023).

Lipsky, M. (1980) *Street Level Bureaucracy – Dilemmas of the Individual in Public Services*, New York, NY: Russell Sage Foundation.

Malm, A. (2020) *Corona, Climate and Chronic Emergency: War Communism in the Twenty-First Century*, London: Verso.

Marston, C., Renedo, A. and Miles, S. (2020) 'Community participation is crucial in a pandemic', *The Lancet* 395: 1676–7.

Martinez-Brawley, E. (1982) *Rural Social Work in the U.S. and Britain*, New York, NY: Praeger.

Martinez-Brawley, E. (1990) *Perspectives on the Small Community*, Washington, DC: NASW Press.

Martinez-Brawley, E. (2000) *Close to Home: Human Services and the Small Community*, Washington, DC: NASW Press.

Mayaka, B., Ulhangana, C. and van Breda, A. (eds) (2023) *The Ubuntu Practitioner – Social Work Perspectives*, Rheinfelden: IFSW.

Mayer, J. and Timms, N. (1970) *The Client Speaks*, London: RKP.

Mayo, M. (2005) *Global Citizens*, London: Earthscan.

McAnee, G. (2023) *Strengthened Connections: Evaluation of a Well-Being Programme Delivered through Community Social Workers in a Primary Care Setting*, Derry: Yellow Wood Consultancy Ltd.

McAnee, G., Ferry, R. and Stack, C. (2021) *Healthy Connections: Evaluation of Clarendon Medical Well-Being Pilot for People with Obesity*, Derry: Western Health & Social Care Trust.

McCulloch, T. and Taylor, S. (2018) 'Becoming a social worker: realising a shared approach to professional learning?', *British Journal of Social Work* 48: 2272–90.

McCulloch, T. and Webb, S. (2020) 'What the public think about social services: a report from Scotland', *British Journal of Social Work* 50(4): 1146–66.

McDonald, C. (2006) *Challenging Social Work – The Context of Practice*, Basingstoke: Palgrave Macmillan.

McGarvey, D. (2018) *Poverty Safari – Understanding the Anger of Britain's Underclass*, London: Picador.

McLafferty Bell, F., Dennis, M.K. and Krings, A. (2019) 'Collective survival strategies and anti-colonial practice in ecosocial work', *Journal of Community Practice* 27(3–4): 279–95.

Miller, E. and Barrie, K. (2022) 'Setting the bar for social work in Scotland', Social Work Scotland https://socialworkscotland.org/wp-content/uploads/2022/05/Setting-the-Bar-Full-Report.pdf (accessed June 2023).

Miller, R., Glasby, J. and Dickinson, H. (2021) 'Integrated health and social care in England – ten years on', *International Journal of Integrated Care* 21(4): 6.

Ministry of Health, Department of Health for Scotland (1959) *Report of the Working Party on Social Workers in the Local Authority and Welfare Services*, London: HMSO.

Ministry of Housing, Communities and Local Government (2020) 'Count of Traveller caravans January 2020, England', https://assets.publishing.service.gov.uk/government/uploads/system/uploads/attachment_data/file/891229/Traveller_caravan_count_2020_stats_release.pdf (accessed August 2023).

Morley, C., Macfarlane, S. and Ablett, P. (2017) 'The neoliberal colonisation of social work education: a critical analysis and practices for resistance', *Advances in Social Work and Welfare Education* 19(2): 25–40.

Morley, C., Ablett, P. and Stenhouse, K. (2019) 'Technicist education; paving the way for the risk of social work robots?', *Critical and Radical Social Work*, 7(2): 139–54.

Mullaly, B. (2010) *Challenging Oppression and Confronting Privilege*, 2nd edn, Ontario: OUP.

Mullender, A. and Ward, D. (1991) *Self-Directed Groupwork: Users Take Action for Empowerment*, London: Whiting & Birch.

Narey, M. (2014) 'Making the education of social workers consistently effective', https://assets.publishing.service.gov.uk/government/uploads/system/uploads/attachment_data/file/287756/Making_the_education_of_social_workers_consistently_effective.pdf (accessed August 2023).

National Audit Office (2017) 'Report – value for money – health and social care integration', https://www.nao.org.uk/reports/health-and-social-care-integration/ (accessed June 2023).

Northern Ireland Department of Health (2018) 'Expansion of community development approaches', https://www.publichea lth.hscni.net/publications/expansion-community-developm ent-approaches (accessed July 2023).

Northern Ireland Department of Health (2019) 'Primary care multi-disciplinary teams', https://www.health-ni.gov.uk/ articles/primary-care-multi-disciplinary-teams-mdts#toc-1 (accessed July 2023).

Northern Ireland Department of Health (2023) *Social Work and Community Development: Reflections*, Belfast: Northern Ireland Department of Health.

Northern Ireland Social Care Council and Department of Health, Social Services and Public Safet. (2015) 'Northern Ireland framework specification for the degree in social work', https:// learningzone.niscc.info/app/uploads/2022/08/The-North ern-Ireland-Framework-Specification-for-the-Degree-2015. pdf (accessed 18 August 2023).

Noyoo, N. (2022) 'Green social work for climate change: curriculum innovations for a post-apartheid South Africa', in Madhanagopal, D. and Nikku, B. (eds) *Social Work and Climate Justice: International Perspectives*, London: Routledge, 155–71.

O'Brien, F., Hawthorne-Steele, I., Pascoe, K.M., Moreland, R., Cownie, E. and Killick, C. (2023) 'Bridging the gap between social work and community development: implementing a post-graduate training partnership', *Social Work Education*, https:// doi.org/10.1080/02615479.2023.2252844

Ofsted (Office for Standards in Education, Children's Services and Skills) (2022) 'Children's social care 2022: recovering from the Covid-19 pandemic', 27 July, https://www.gov.uk/gov ernment/publications/childrens-social-care-2022-recovering-from-the-covid-19-pandemic/childrens-social-care-2022-rec overing-from-the-covid-19-pandemic (accessed May 2023).

Ohmer, M. and Korr, W. (2006) 'The effectiveness of community practice interventions: a review of the literature', *Research on Social Work Practice* 16(2): 132–45.

Oprescu, F., Fjaagesund, S., Hardy, M. and Jones, E. (February 2023) 'Transforming primary care: developing health precincts as models for sustainable integrated community-based healthcare', *Healthcare* 11(5): 673.

Parker, J. (2020) 'Descent or dissent? A future of social work education in the UK post-Brexit', *European Journal of Social Work* 23(5): 837–48.

Perlman, H. (1957) *Social Casework: A Problem Solving Process*, Chicago, IL: Chicago University Press.

Pierson, J. (2008) *Going Local – Working in Communities and Neighbourhoods*, Abington: Routledge.

Pierson, J. (2021) *A New History of Social Work: Values and Practice in the Struggle for Social Justice*, Abingdon: Routledge.

Pincus, A. and Minahan, A. (1973) *Social Work Practice: Model and Method*, Itasca, IL: Peacock.

Prochaska, J. and DiClemente, C. (1983) 'Stages and processes of self-change of smoking: toward an integrative model of change', *Journal of Consulting and Clinical Psychology* 51(3): 390–5.

Prynn, B. and Rapaport, J. (2009) 'Forty years since Seebohm', *Professional Social Work*, February.

Pye, J. and Turbett, C. (eds) (2024) *Rural Social Work in the UK – Themes and Challenges for the Future*, London: Palgrave.

QAA (Quality Assurance Agency for Higher Education) (2019) 'Subject benchmark statement social work', https://www.qaa.ac.uk/docs/qaa/subject-benchmark-statements/subject-benchmark-statement-social-work.pdf?sfvrsn=5c35c881_8 (accessed August 2023).

Rao, S., Teixeira, S. and Billiot, S. (2023) 'Social work and environmental justice – expanding critical social work', in Webb, S. (ed) *The Routledge Handbook of International Critical Social Work – New Perspectives and Agendas*, London: Routledge, 643–59.

Redcliffe, J. and Ortiz, J. (2023) 'Social work education in Wales', in Livingston W., Redcliffe, J. and Quinn, A. (eds) *Social Work in Wales*, Bristol: Policy Press, 57–69.

Rogowski, S. (2010) *Social Work: The Rise and Fall of a Profession?*, Bristol: Policy Press.

Rogowski, S. (2020) *Social Work: The Rise and Fall of a Profession?*, 2nd edn, Bristol: Policy Press.

Ruch, G., Turney, D. and Ward, A. (2018) *Relationship Based Social Work – Getting to the Heart of Practice*, 2nd edn, London: Jessica Kingsley.

Russell, C. (2016) 'From what's wrong to what's strong: a guide to community-driven development', https://socialworkwithadu lts.blog.gov.uk/2016/04/29/community-social-work-the-shift-from-whats-wrong-to-whats-strong/ (accessed June 2023).

Russell, C. and McKnight, J. (2022) *The Connected Community – Discovering the Health, Wealth and Power of Neighbourhoods*, Oakland, CA: Berret-Koehler.

Schön, D. (1991) *The Reflective Practitioner – How Professionals Think in Action*, Abingdon: Routledge.

Scottish Education Department, Scottish Home and Health Department (1966) *Social Work and the Community*, Cmnd 3065, Edinburgh: HMSO.

Scottish Government (2011) 'Commission on the Future Delivery of Public Services (Christie Commission Report)', https://www.gov.scot/publications/commission-future-delivery-pub lic-services/ (accessed July 2023).

Scottish Government (2021) 'The independent review of adult social care (Feeley Report)', https://www.gov.scot/groups/independent-review-of-adult-social-care/ (accessed July 2023).

Scottish Government (2023) 'National Care Service (Scotland) Bill', https://www.parliament.scot/bills-and-laws/bills/natio nal-care-service-scotland-bill (accessed July 2023).

SCW (Social Care Wales) (2011) 'National occupational standards – social work', https://socialcare.wales/resources-guida nce/early-years-and-childcare/national-occupational-standards-nos/social-work (accessed August 2023).

SCW (2019) 'The social worker – practice guidance for social workers registered with Social Care Wales', https://socialcare. wales/cms-assets/documents/Practice-guidance-social-workers. pdf (accessed August 2023).

SCW (2021a) 'The framework for the degree in social work in Wales 2021', https://socialcare.wales/cms-assets/docume nts/Framework-for-social-work-degree-2021.pdf (accessed August 2023).

SCW (2021b) 'The Wales framework for the social work degree: supplementary guidance to the rules', https://socialc are.wales/cms-assets/documents/Supplementary-Guidance-to-the-Rules-2021.pdf (accessed August 2023).

SCW (2022) 'Social Services and Well-Being (Wales) Act 2014 – overview', https://socialcare.wales/resources-guidance/informat ion-and-learning-hub/sswbact/overview (accessed July 2023).

Seebohm, F. (1968) *Report of the Committee on Local Authority and Allied Personal Services*, London: HMSO.

Shaw, M. (2011 [2008]) 'Community development and the politics of community', in Craig, G., Mayo, M., Popple, K., Shaw, M. and Taylor, M. (eds) *The Community Development Reader – History, Themes and Issues*, Bristol: Policy Press, 301–308.

Simey, T. (1947) *Salaries and Conditions of Social Workers – A Report by a Joint Committee under the Chairmanship of T.S. Simey M.A.*, London: National Council of Social Service.

Smale, G. and Bennett, W. (eds) (1989) *Pictures of Practice Vol. 1: Community Social Work in Scotland*, London: NISW.

Smale, G., Tuson, G., Cooper, M., Wardle, M. and Crosbie, D. (1988) *Community Social Work: A Paradigm for Change*, London: NISW.

Smale, G., Tuson, G. and Statham, D. (2000) *Social Work and Social Problems – Working towards Social Inclusion and Social Change*, Basingstoke: Macmillan.

Smart Transport (2023) 'What is a 15-minute neighbourhood?', https://www.smarttransport.org.uk/insight-and-policy/lat est-insight-and-policy/what-is-a-15-minute-neighbourhood (accessed April 2023).

Smith, K. (2022) 'Climate change and macro social work', in Franklin, C. (ed) *Encyclopaedia of Social Work*, https://global.oup. com/academic/product/encyclopedia-of-social-work-978019 9975839?cc=gb&lang=en& (accessed January 2024).

Smith, L. (2018) *Iriss ESSS Outline – Capturing Social Work Impact*, Glasgow: Iriss.

Smith, M. and Whyte, B. (2008) 'Social education and social pedagogy: reclaiming a Scottish tradition in social work', *European Journal of Social Work* 11(1): 15–28.

SSSC (Scottish Social Services Council) (2019) 'Standards in social work education in Scotland', https://learn.sssc.uk.com/ siswe/uploads/files/SiSWE-and-Ethical-Principles.pdf (accessed August 2023).

Stephenson, F. and Stephenson, G. (1942) *Community Centres – A Survey*, London: National Council of Social Service.

Stepney, P. and Ford, D. (2000) *Social Work Models, Methods and Theories – A Framework for Practice*, Lyme Regis: RHP.

Stepney, P. and Popple, K. (2008) *Social Work and the Community – A Critical Context for Practice*, Basingstoke: Palgrave Macmillan.

SWE (Social Work England) (2019) 'Professional standards', https://www.socialworkengland.org.uk/media/1640/1227_socialworkengland_standards_prof_standards_final-aw.pdf (accessed August 2023).

SWE (2021) 'Education and training standards', https://www.socialworkengland.org.uk/standards/education-and-training-standards/ (accessed August 2023).

SWE (2022) 'Consultation on readiness for professional practice', https://www.socialworkengland.org.uk/about/consultations/consultation-on-readiness-for-professional-practice/ (accessed August 2023).

SWEP (Social Work Education Partnership – Scotland) (2022) 'Infrastructure to enable development of the future social work workforce', SWEP Programme Office, Social Work Scotland.

Teater, B. and Baldwin, M. (2012) *Social Work in the Community – Making a Difference*, Bristol: Policy Press.

The Guardian (2011) 'Dale Farm evictions – complete timeline', 19 October, https://www.theguardian.com/uk/2011/oct/19/dale-farm-evictions-complete-timeline (accessed August 2023).

The Guardian (2012) 'Big Fat Gypsy Weddings has increased bullying of Gypsies and Travellers', 16 October, https://www.theguardian.com/media/2012/oct/16/big-fat-gypsy-weddings-bullying-travellers (accessed August 2023).

The Guardian (2016) 'Bob Holman – obituary', 15 June, https://www.theguardian.com/society/2016/jun/15/bob-holman-obituary (accessed July 2023).

The Guardian (2021) '"A massive injustice": 10 years on from Dale Farm evictions, pain and trauma remain', 21 October, https://www.theguardian.com/uk-news/2021/oct/21/a-massive-injustice-ten-years-on-from-dale-farm-traveller-site-essex-evictions-pain-and-trauma-remain (accessed August 2023).

Tight, M. (2002) 'Do league tables contribute to the development of a quality culture? Football and higher education compared', *Higher Education Quarterly* 54(1): 22–43.

Tobis, D., Bilson, A. and Katugampala, I. (2020) *International Review of Parent Advocacy in Child Welfare: Strengthening Children's Care and Protection through Parent Participation*, New York, NY: Better Care Network & IPAN.

Turbett, C. (2010) *Rural Social Work Practice in Scotland*, Birmingham: Venture Press.

Turbett, C. (2013) 'Radical social work in the frontline: a survival toolkit for the UK', *Critical & Radical Social Work* 1(2): 225–32.

Turbett, C. (2014) *Doing Radical Social Work*, Basingstoke: Palgrave Macmillan.

Turbett, C. (2018a) *Social Work across the UK – Legal and Policy Differences from a Scottish Perspective*, Edinburgh: SASW, https://www.basw.co.uk/system/files/resources/Acrobat%20Document.pdf (accessed July 2023).

Turbett, C. (2018b) 'Community social work in Scotland – a critical history', https://www.iriss.org.uk/resources/reports/community-social-work-scotland (accessed August 2023).

Turbett, C. (2020) 'Rediscovering and mainstreaming community social work in Scotland', Iriss Insight 57, https://www.iriss.org.uk/resources/insights/rediscovering-and-mainstreaming-community-social-work-scotland (accessed August 2023).

Turbett, C. (2021a) 'Struggling to care – why Scotland needs to reform the role of social workers', https://commonweal.scot/policies/struggling-to-care/ (accessed August 2023).

Turbett, C. (2021b) 'Care in your community – putting community hubs at the heart of a national care service', https://commonweal.scot/wp-content/uploads/2021/06/Community-Hubs.pdf (accessed May 2023).

Turbett, C. (2023a) 'From welfare to charity – the Scottish Government, local government and the third sector', https://commonweal.scot/policies/from-welfare-to-charity/ (accessed May 2023).

Turbett, C. (2023b) 'How critical theory informs radical social work practice', in Webb, S. (ed) *The Routledge Handbook of International Critical Social Work – New Perspectives and Agendas*, Abingdon: Routledge, 119–31.

UK Government (1968) *Report of the Committee on Local Authority and Allied Personal Social Services (Seebohm Report)*, Cmnd 3703, London: HMSO.

UK Government (2014) 'Care Act 2014 Part 1 Section 2', https://www.legislation.gov.uk/ukpga/2014/23/section/2/enacted (accessed July 2023).

UK Government (2021) 'Policy Paper: Supporting Families – 2021–22 and beyond', https://www.gov.uk/government/publications/supporting-families-2021-to-2022-and-beyond/supporting-families-2021-22-and-beyond (accessed July 2023).

UK Government (2022) 'The independent review of children's social care – final report', https://www.gov.uk/government/publications/independent-review-of-childrens-social-care-final-report (accessed July 2023).

UK Government (2023) 'Children Act 1989', https://www.legislation.gov.uk/ukpga/1989/41/ (accessed July 2023).

UK Parliament (2023) 'Levelling Up and Regeneration Bill', https://bills.parliament.uk/bills/3155 (accessed July 2023).

UNISON Scotland (2014) 'Supervision and workload management for social work – a negotiating resource', https://unison-scotland.org/supervision-and-workload-management/ (accessed May 2023).

UNISON Scotland (2019) 'Save from harm – UNISON Scotland survey of social work teams', https://unison-scotland.org/save-from-harm/ (accessed June 2023).

United Nations (2023) 'The 17 Sustainable Development Goals', https://sdgs.un.org/goals#history (accessed January 2024).

Wales Care Inspectorate (2019) 'Inspection of older adult services Torfaen County Borough Council', https://www.careinspectorate.wales/sites/default/files/2019-10/191004-inspection-of-Older-adults-services-torfaen-county-borough-council-en.pdf (accessed August 2023).

Webb, S. (ed) (2023) *The Routledge Handbook of International Critical Social Work – New Perspectives and Agendas*, Abingdon: Routledge.

Webber, F. (2012) *Borderline Justice: The Fight for Refugee and Migrant Rights*, London: Pluto Press.

Welsh Government (2020) 'Social Services and Well-being (Wales) Act 2014 codes and guidance: Part 9 statutory guidance (partnership arrangements), January 2020, Version 2', https://www.gov.wales/sites/default/files/publications/2020-02/part-9-statutory-guidance-partnership-arrangements.pdf (accessed August 2020).

Welsh Government (2022) 'Expectations and experiences: service user and carer perspectives on the Social Services and Well-being (Wales) Act', https://www.gov.wales/sites/default/files/statist ics-and-research/2022-03/expectations-and-experiences-serv ice-user-and-carer-perspectives-on-the-social-services-and-well-being-wales-act.pdf (accessed July 2023).

Welsh Government (2023) 'Regional partnership boards: charter for service user, carer, third sector and provider members, February 2023', https://www.gov.wales/regional-partners hip-boards-charter-service-user-carer-third-sector-and-provi der-members-html-0 (accessed July 2023).

Westoby, P., Lathouras, A. and Shevellar, A. (2019) 'Radicalising community development within social work through popular education – a participatory action research project', *British Journal of Social Work* 49(8): 2207–25.

Whelan, J. (2022) 'From dissent to authoritarianism: what role for social work in confronting the climate crisis?', *Aotearoa New Zealand Social Work* 34(3): 21–33.

Which? Online (2019) 'Three food waste facts everyone needs to know', https://www.which.co.uk/news/article/three-food-waste-facts-everyone-needs-to-know-aIHRD3H1gpEv (accessed January 2023).

Wilkinson, R. and Pickett, K. (2010) *The Spirit Level – Why Equality is Better for Everyone*, London: Penguin.

Worsley, A. (2023) 'Moving the river: rethinking regulation in social work', *British Journal of Social Work* 43: 2352–69.

Wroe, L., Larkin, R. and Maglajlic, R. (eds) (2019) *Social Work with Refugees, Asylum Seekers and Migrants – Theory and Skills for Practice*, London: Jessica Kingsley.

Younghusband, E. (1947) *Report on the Employment and Training of Social Workers*, Edinburgh: Carnegie Trust/Constable.

Younghusband, E. (1964) *Social Work and Social Change*, National Institute for Social Work Training Series No. 1, London: George Allen & Unwin.

Younghusband, E. (1968) *Community Work and Social Change – The Report of a Study Group on Training Set up by the Calouste Gulbenkian Foundation*, London: Longman.

Index

Printed and bound by CPI Group (UK) Ltd, Croydon, CR0 4YY

25/03/2025

14647337-0002